Witches and Witchcraft

Witches and Witchcraft

By the Editors of Time-Life Books

TIME-LIFE BOOKS, ALEXANDRIA, VIRGINIA

CONTENTS

CHAPTER 1

From Goddess to Flying Hag

isitors to the rugged coast of Scotland east of Edinburgh will sometimes catch wind of a peculiar legend about strange goings-on long ago in the village of North Berwick. The story tends to vary in its details from one telling to the next, but its actors are always portrayed the same, as a thoroughly sinister band of witches. If the tale is to be believed—and here, some caution is necessary—in the autumn of 1590, a group of wicked men and women came together to perform a hideous ritual in an empty church not far from the North Sea. The ambitions of the witches were both grand and terrible, for they planned to seize control of the forces of nature and to change the course of Scottish history by raising a terrible storm at sea.

In the small church, the witches huddled about the form of a frightened cat, chosen as the agent of their magic. First, they christened the unfortunate animal in a ritual ceremony, then tortured it cruelly, passing it back and forth across a flaming hearth. Next, they affixed the hands and feet of a dead man, whose body they had stolen from a nearby cemetery, to the cat's paws and attached the sex organs from the dismembered corpse to the cat's underside. This done, the witches carried their gruesome offering to a pier at the nearby village of Leith and flung it into the sea.

At once, the story goes, a terrible storm arose, turning the skies black and sending up a howling wind across the churning sea. A ship making the crossing from Kinghorn to Leith was engulfed in the squall and smashed to pieces, killing many sailors. This tragedy did little, however, to satisfy the blood lust of the Berwick witches. Their target was a different vessel. That night, a royal man-of-war was scheduled to make passage from Denmark to Scotland. On board, along with his bride, was His Royal Majesty King James VI of Scotland, who later became King James I of England. To the consternation of the Berwick coven, the king's ship escaped destruction. They would have to find other measures.

The story of the attempted murder of the king came to light shortly thereafter, during an investigation of suspected witchcraft in the Edinburgh area. A young servant girl named Gilly Duncan, who was known for her skills in nursing the sick, had confessed to evoking the aid of the devil to enhance her powers. That this admission had been divulged under severe torture made little difference to anyone; such measures were standard practice in cases involving witchcraft. Poor Gilly was forced to name her accomplices, and she implicated nearly seventy of Edinburgh's most prominent citizens.

When the girl's testimony came to the attention of the king, he decided to listen in on the interrogations of the other accused witches. He began with Agnes Sampson, a grave and matronly gentlewoman.

Agnes refused to confess to any crime, so her jailers went to work. First her body was stripped, shaved, and searched for an incriminating devil's mark—a mole or other blemish from which witches supposedly allowed the Evil One to suck blood from their limbs. When a mark was found, the next step was torture. The jailers tied a rough rope contraption around Agnes Sampson's neck and, by jerking it harshly, made painful abrasions in the flesh. They then forced an iron "witch's bridle" into the old woman's mouth, so that two prongs pressed into her tongue and two others gouged her cheeks. In this condition, she was permitted no sleep, and after several days, she too began to talk.

As the words poured out, James listened. Agnes said anything that came into her head. Not only had she used charms to cure disease, she admitted to keeping her own private devil, or familiar spirit—a dog whom she called Elva. More to the point, from the king's perspective, she described a gathering that she had attended with ninety other women and six men. The company had fueled up on wine, then made its way to the church at North Berwick, where they worshiped Satan with chants and obscene kisses. Black candles lighted the church, and Gilly Duncan played a merry tune on a Jew's harp. (The credulous James was so entranced by this last feature that he had Gilly and her harp brought to him for a command performance.)

The confession continued with an account of the ritual with the cat and the plot on the life of the king. When James recalled that his voyage to Scotland had been uncommonly rough, he reached the conclusion that he was indeed in mortal danger from these godless miscreants. Agnes was condemned to death and burned at the stake. Along with her, Gilly Duncan and two others were executed. James, who considered himself something of a scholar, wrote a treatise, *Demonology,* based on his observations. Then in 1603, at the death of his cousin, Elizabeth I of England, he became monarch of that country as well. The witchcraft statutes of England were woefully lenient in his opinion, so James decided to stiffen the laws and thus helped launch a number of notable witch trials in this country.

What, if anything, actually transpired in the old church at North Berwick is now impossible to know. Most scholars dismiss confessions like those of Gilly Duncan and Agnes Sampson, which were given under extreme duress. Many historians, moreover, scoff at the notion of sorcerers supposedly in league with the devil attempting a murder by raising a storm at sea. There are, in addition, many other skeptics who reject the Berwick story even though they place great faith in the efficacy of magic. Among the last group are modern-day witches, who would argue that the Berwick tale impugns the character of their long-ago forebears in the towns, forests, and farmlands of Scotland.

Modern witches—and there are today growing numbers of people studying the traditions of magic and witchcraft—feel that the Berwick legend is typical of a great mass of anecdotal evidence that has wrongly been accepted as historical fact and has colored our assumptions about witchcraft. They believe, with some justification, that the court records assembled by witch prosecutors over the centuries paint a grossly unfair image of their mysterious predecessors in times gone by. Underlying their objections is a sense that the Berwick story, like many others, transforms into the Christian devil the gods of simple people like Gilly Duncan, who were, in all likelihood, not evildoers but pa-

gans. Modern witches contend that many of the victims of the witchcraft tribunals were holdovers of a religion that was deeply entrenched in Europe before the spread of Christianity. And they state that just as in many comparable tales, the Berwick legend interprets the motives of the Scottish pagans as predictably evil, rather than presuming that such people might have been good and well intentioned.

Perhaps the legend is typical. Like most old witch stories, it describes a wicked plot and an ominous magic spell set in motion by depraved and secretive people. More than this, it reflects a vivid and fanciful notion of witches that has carried over into our highly stereotyped image of witchcraft today. That image was far more fearsome and richly detailed in the late sixteenth century, when the Berwick episode allegedly took place.

In the time of James VI, witches were thought to be worshipers of Satan. They were considered dangerous even in isolation but were deemed all the more menacing because they had been organized into a collective body of anti-Christians, bound together by communal rites and held in subservience by the devil. Witches were not perceived as having been born into such perversity. Precisely the opposite: They were heretics, fallen-away Christians, who had been trapped individually by the Evil One himself and then coerced into participating in sacrilegious observances that turned the Christian liturgy on its head.

People taught their children that Satan drew his disciples from ordinary folk and that he usually found them when they needed him most—when they were impoverished, bereaved, sick, or discouraged. The prospective witch was most often a woman, but men were recruited too and the

Satan directs his minions from a hollow tree in this 1591 woodcut of the North Berwick witches. At top left, a ship is battered by the storm that witches at top right are brewing up in a cauldron; at center, the coven's secretary takes notes; at bottom, the witches celebrate in a wine cellar.

occasional child as well. Satan was cunningly unpredictable in the ways that he wooed new converts. He might first show himself as an animal or perhaps would assume a human appearance and wear the clothes of a nobleman or priest. Always he made promises: for the orphan, a home; for the widow, a lover; for the drought-stricken farmer, a spring. But hard behind the promises were threats and demands for loyalty and obedience. And even when the promises were broken—when the home turned out to be horrible or the long-awaited spring dried up—the demands remained in effect. Eventually, Satan forced his candidates to enter into pacts with him. The new witches would renounce God and promise unending allegiance to the devil.

From that day forth, the witches were encouraged to make life miserable for Christians. *Maleficium* was the term

of the day for evil performed by occult means, and to make his witches a potent source of upheaval, Satan gave them supernatural powers. Witches could transform themselves into frogs, ravens, or fireflies or even make themselves invisible. They tormented their neighbors by ruining crops, killing cattle, and snuffing out the lives of human babies not yet out of the womb. Satan's workers also used magic to spread impotence, sterility, illness, insanity, and death.

Periodically, Satan called upon his troops to attend meetings known as sabbats. To get to the site of these convocations—usually at crossroads deep in the woods or on mountaintops in distant lands—the witches would slip from the beds of their unwitting husbands or wives, perhaps leaving behind an enchanted stick that would assume their appearance, should the spouse awake. Then the devil's followers would slather themselves with a magic salve rendered from the flesh of murdered children and fly to the sabbat on the back of a pig, a fence rail, or a broomstick. Once arrived, they joined Satan in wicked parodies of the Christian sacraments and engaged in every form of human degradation, from cannibalism to bestiality to incest.

Whether or not this diabolical form of witchcraft was ever practiced by actual people is debated among historians. Some say that it never was or that if there were isolated pockets of devil worshipers, they were probably extremely rare. Nonetheless, this lurid and threatening view of the witch held force in Europe for many centuries and had immense consequences on the lives of the Continent's inhabitants. At various times, concern about diabolical witchcraft boiled over into religious hysteria. The most notorious example was the prolonged witch craze of the fifteenth, sixteenth, and seventeenth centuries. During this time, accused witches numbering in the hundreds of thousands were put to death. Many of them were guilty of no crime more heinous than provoking a neighbor's jealousy. And most were condemned on the basis of confessions no more valid or enlightening than those of Gilly Duncan and Agnes Sampson.

The stereotyped image of sons and daughters of Satan that moved King James and sparked the great European witch craze is in stark contrast to the image cherished by modern practitioners of witchcraft. Today's witches see themselves as part of a revival of an ancient nature religion—one they say predates Christianity and has no particular stake in opposing the teachings of Jesus. The religion, called Wicca, is linked to the seasons, and rather than being fixated on wickedness and maleficium, it is, by and large, mirthful and celebratory. It venerates an ancient female deity called the Mother Goddess, who, in her many incarnations, has been worshiped in agricultural societies since time immemorial. Some branches of Wicca also revere a male deity, connected with the ancient Horned God, lord of the hunt and lord of death. In the eyes of the Wiccans, the Horned God is unrelated to the figure of Satan.

The discrepancy between the historical stereotype of the witch and the concepts of the Wiccans today highlights the fact that the image of a witch has always been highly changeable. The concept of diabolical witchcraft was formalized in a somewhat piecemeal fashion by the Church of Rome, during the Middle Ages, as it struggled to consolidate its rather tenuous foothold in Europe. Raising the threat of witchcraft proved useful to the Church, both in rooting out heretical challengers to the centralized leadership of Rome, and in smothering the remnants of the pagan religions that continued to flourish on the Continent. But the Church fathers did not have to start from scratch in cooking up the specter of anti-Christian devil worshipers. Rather, they were able to improvise on an old recipe, adding a few new ingredients to a long-simmering stew of superstition and fear. The image of the witch before the Church married her to Satan was the product of many influences—including pagan religious practices, folklore, and the commonplace acceptance of the power of magic among Europeans.

Perhaps the most deep-seated influence, though, was the power of the mythologies that shaped every aspect of thought and belief within the European cultures. The mythologies of the Near East, Greece, Rome, and northern Europe are heavily laden with higher and lower beings who embody the traits and practice the arts later attributed to witches. A few of the myths that gave shape to the perception of witchcraft have been passed down from the very earliest of human societies. Most important of these is the deeply held tale of a profoundly ambivalent figure called the Mother Goddess.

No one knows with certainty when people first began to worship a mother goddess. There is tantalizing evidence, however, that the belief may have arisen at the very dawn of our species, sometime late in the so-called Paleolithic period, when *Homo neanderthalensis* gave way to *Homo sapiens*. Whereas the cave paintings of that distant time depict mostly animals, with the few images of men hidden behind masks in a manner that suggests some magical activity, almost all of the sculptures that remain show women. About 130 carvings, worked in stone, bone, and the ivory tusks of the mammoth, have been discovered over a wide geographical area from France in the west to Siberia in the east and from Willendorf in Austria to the Balkans in southeastern Europe. Called Venus figurines, they seem to speak of a female deity and of the magical powers of women.

The Venuses are highly stylized renderings of the female form. Some of them strongly resemble modern art—no surprise, since they captured the imagination of many nineteenth- and twentieth-century artists, who saw them on exhibit in European museums. The subjects are usually naked, generally obese, and all but faceless in their lack of detail. Their exaggerated hips, breasts, and pubic triangles make them more symbols of the womanly power to bear new life than depictions of actual women. Some examples show the distended belly of a woman in pregnancy.

The use of these ancient carvings in religious observance has never been conclusively proved. In fact, because the artists placed such emphasis on their suggestions of fertility and sexuality, some anthropologists have dismissed the statuettes as nothing more than erotic art—or, at best, simple good-luck charms for couples hoping to conceive.

But in recent years, scholars have attributed to the Venuses much more significance than that. The noted mythologist Joseph Campbell, for one, considered them proof that—even in the Stone Age—the female body was revered as a focus of divine force. Pointing out that a few of the figurines were excavated in what appeared to be shrines and that all of them were carved without feet so they could be stuck reverently upright in the ground, Campbell referred to the Venuses as the very earliest works of religious art. He saw two possible explanations for these mysterious carvings, either of which would seem to shed light on much later beliefs about witchcraft.

The first possibility is that the cult of the Mother Goddess, which is generally associated with later agricultural civilizations, somehow took seed in the earliest human societies of hunters and gatherers. Alternatively, the Venus figurines can be looked upon as the first artistic expression of the timeless theme of woman as the giver of life. In either case, a profoundly important and yet disturbing idea had made its way into the human psyche. As Joseph Campbell explained: "There can be no doubt that in the very earliest ages of human history the magical force and wonder of the female was no less a marvel than the universe itself; and this gave to woman a prodigious power, which it has been one of the chief concerns of the masculine part of the population to break, control, and employ to its own ends."

The effects of this primordial wedge in the relationship of males and females would play themselves out in the mythologies of many cultures to follow. In real-world terms, moreover, the same tension would contribute to devastating upheavals such as the great European witch hunt.

he full flowering of the cult of the Mother Goddess awaited the more advanced agricultural societies of the Neolithic period. By the fifth millennium BC, the peoples of the Near East began to settle into village life and to establish a farming economy. People learned to sow wheat and barley and to domesticate animals such as goats, sheep, pigs, and oxen. Skills such as weaving, pottery-making, and carpentry also were refined in this time. One result of these changes was a dramatically enhanced role for women in society. In the hunting cultures of the preceding centuries, women had been revered for their power to bear childen, but they were limited mainly to drudge work in their communities, while men provided most of the sustenance. Now, women supplied both the babies and food, as they took charge of the planting and the reaping. In the minds of both males and females, women became symbolically linked to earth in its productivity.

A multitude of figurines exist from the High Neolithic period, which extends from 4500 to 3500 BC, and these carvings show a much more clear-cut religious intent than the Paleolithic Venuses. Another 2,000 years would pass before writing was invented, but even without written documentation, scholars are able to make an educated guess about the role of the Neolithic figurines. Their function, it

Companions in Evil: The Cat

No storybook witch would be complete without a black cat, her steady companion and accomplice in evil doings. Not that cats were the only animals associated with witches. Far from it: Ferrets, rabbits, hedgehogs, blackbirds, owls, crows, toads, and frogs were all considered suitable helpmates for sorceresses. (The folk traditions surrounding two of these so-called familiars—toads and owls—are discussed on pages 14 and 15.)

Cats and other alleged familiars frequently served as evidence in British witch trials of the seventeenth century, a custom that had the unfortunate side effect of lowering a pall of suspicion over people who formed close attachments to their pets. Animals had played many roles in the pagan myths and religious practices of Europe, and some of the superstitions about the magical capacities of small creatures survived when the Continent became Christianized. Church doctrine was developed that encouraged the credulous to discern the shadow of Satan in any strong relationship with an animal.

Cat lovers were particularly vulnerable to suspicion because of the longstanding superstitions about felines. No less than four thousand years ago, cats had been worshiped in Egypt as sacred animals and revered by religious cults. In the city of Bubastis, festivals celebrating the cat-headed goddess, Bast, included music, dancing, and sexual rituals. The affection of the Egyptians for cats probably stemmed from a recognition that the animals had value in protecting granaries from vermin. But the affinity was deeply felt, and anyone who killed a cat was subject to execution. A contemporary account tells of a Roman in Egypt who was slain by a mob in his own home for killing a cat.

Other parts of the ancient world also attached religious significance to cats. The Roman goddess Diana was said to assume a feline form, and in northern Europe, cats drew the chariot of Freya, the goddess of love and beauty. The advent of Christianity in Europe brought an end to the veneration. Eager to repudiate every aspect of paganism, the Church taught that the formerly sacred animals were minor demons. And as the Church fathers fought to stamp out heretical sects, they at times made reference to feline superstitions in describing the dangers posed by dissenters. The Cathars, for example, were accused of worshiping the devil in the form of a cat.

With the coming of the European witch hunt, the forced confessions of alleged witches were used to back up the Church's claims. A white-spotted cat named Sathan became a featured player in the 1566 English trial of Elizabeth Francis. Sathan, the prosecutors declared, had performed many magical services for Francis. The cat had filled up his mistress's pastures with sheep and brought her suitors. Sathan was credited with killing a suitor after the match turned sour. And each time Sathan aided Francis, witnesses said, he was rewarded with a drop of her blood.

At a trial in 1618, a cat was portrayed as having figured in the magic that sent Margaret and Philippa Flower to the gallows (see page 61). Margaret confessed to having rubbed the gloves of her intended victims on the belly of her pet. The fate of Margaret's cat is not recorded, but most familiars of convicted witches were burned alive.

This mummified cat is one of hundreds of thousands discovered in Egyptian cat cemeteries, often in the company of mouse mummies that presumably served as food in the afterlife. The care taken in wrapping the body and the elaborately painted face attest to the regard Egyptians had for cats. Some mummies were interred in intricate cases of wood or bronze.

would seem, was not terribly different from that of religious art today. They were collected in household shrines to inspire prayer or to focus the mind during meditation. They were prized for their decorative value and for the protection they might bring to the home. To women in childbirth, the statues were magical assistance—if only psychological. And to the farmers, who carried them into the fields, they were luck for the harvest and insurance for the livestock.

The goddess depicted in the Neolithic carvings is multifaceted and changeable. First and foremost a mother, she might be shown squatting in childbirth, offering her breasts with her hands, or pointing a finger to her genitals. But she also personified the earth and might just as well be shown with her plants and animals. Various figurines represent the goddess clutching bunches of flowers, communing with lions and goats, and riding on the backs and horns of bulls. From the start, she was perceived as a paradox. She was the giver of life, but also the one who must take everything away. Within her purview fell the entire cycle of human existence. She was, in the memorable phrase of Joseph Campbell, "the womb and the tomb: the sow that eats her farrow." While her images might capture her reaching out with welcoming arms, they might also show her holding forth the serpents of destruction.

Sometime around 4000 BC, people we now call Sumerians began to settle on the mud flats of the Tigris and Euphrates rivers. There they cultivated the fertile soil of Mesopotamia, which each year was refreshed by the flooding rivers. The Sumerians discovered how to make sun-dried bricks out of mud, and they used such blocks, among other things, to construct the earliest known temples.

These structures took the stairstep pyramid shape of the ziggurat, reaching upward so that the goddess of the earth could be symbolically united with the deities of the skies. In some areas, Sumerian farming villages grew in size and began to function as market centers, and from such beginnings, kingly cities arose with names such as Ur, Eridu, Sippar, and Nippur. In each city, the local queen or princess came to be identified with the goddess.

Over the next 1,500 years, the advances of the Sumerians were repeated and surpassed by peoples throughout the Near East—from Anatolia in the north to Egypt in the south and from the Mediterranean coast to Iran. In all of these places, the goddess was the dominant mythic form. She was the personification of time, space, and matter within whom all life found beginning and end. The spark of life, she was also the substance of which plants and bodies were made and the receiver of the dead in an unending cycle of reincarnation. Her names and the functions attributed to her by individual cultures within the Middle East became highly intertwined as commerce grew throughout the region. In Egypt, she was identified with the creation myth and the goddess Nut, and with Nut's offspring Isis, who used magic to salvage new life following the death of her husband-brother Osiris. In Sumeria, she was called Inanna and Ereshkigal; in Babylon, Ishtar and Tiamat; and in the land of Canaan, she was Astarte or Anat.

Had the mythologies that helped form the cultures of Europe somehow frozen at this point, the concept of the witch in the time of the great persecutions would undoubtedly have been much different. It is possible, in fact, that we might now all share the Wiccan view of witchcraft as a life-giving and nurturing art. Already, however, a profound change had begun in the image of the goddess, which had been brought about by a prolonged period of invasions in the sphere of the Great Mother.

From the deserts to the south came warring tribes of Semites, former hunters who were, by the fourth millennium BC, herders of goats and sheep. From Europe and southern Russia came waves of Hellenic and Aryan invaders, who were cattle grazers and were likewise descendants of hunting civilizations. These intruders conquered the cities of the farming cultures and did their best to banish the essentially harmonious, nonheroic view of nature in which the goddess had thrived. The intruders suppressed the mythologies of the Mother Goddess and reinterpreted her character in the process of installing their own firmaments of

Companions: The Toad

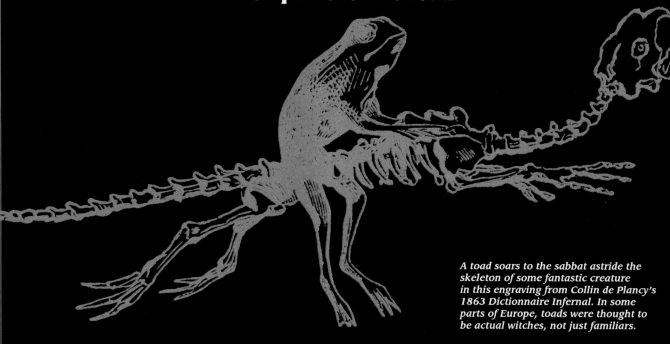

A toad soars to the sabbat astride the skeleton of some fantastic creature in this engraving from Collin de Plancy's 1863 Dictionnaire Infernal. In some parts of Europe, toads were thought to be actual witches, not just familiars.

Though never worshiped like cats, toads, too, have long been associated with mysterious powers. Some nine thousand years ago, artisans were crafting stone and clay images of the Mother Goddess in the shape of a toad. The ancient Greeks and Romans believed that the creatures had the ability to predict or affect the weather. In the first century AD, the Roman naturalist Pliny the Elder advised farmers to avert storms by putting toads inside earthenware pots and placing the pots in their fields. He also cautioned, however, that the animals were ''full of poison.''

Two centuries later, the Roman writer Aelian stated that a mixture of toad blood and wine produced a fatal poison—an exaggeration that was nonetheless grounded in reality. When irritated, toads secrete a venomous fluid that makes dogs foam at the mouth and become feverish. But only in extreme cases is the poison deadly.

The toad's sinister image was bolstered by the repute of this venom, by the amphibian's natural love of dank places, and by its disconcerting face, which resembles that of a grotesque human. By the Middle Ages, the toad was deemed a favorite of witches, serving as a familiar and as a source of ingredients for magic potions. Toad spittle, for example, was considered an essential component in a concoction that supposedly bestowed invisibility.

Witches were believed to be especially fond of their toad companions. One particularly colorful report detailed how the creatures were pampered like children and dressed in scarlet silk, with green velvet capes and bells around their necks. Thus adorned, the toads were then baptized in the name of Satan at the sabbat.

asserts the connection of the Great Mother to nature and rebirth, at a time when her character was more often portrayed as deathly.

Such darker aspects were stressed in Greece, where the cult of the Mother Goddess probably had made its way via the distinct cultures of Crete and Cyprus. In writings published in the 1920s, the English mythologist Jane Ellen Harrison cited elements of the later mystery cults and field festivals of classical Greece that showed that a female deity had for a time ruled supreme among the gods and goddesses of pre-Homeric mythology. The goddess was not, however, the life-giving mother figure worshiped in ancient Mesopotamia. Rather, she was dark and ominous. Her consort was generally depicted as a snake and the offerings made to her on feast days were pigs slaughtered in the gloom of the forests. In Harrison's words: ''The beings worshiped were not rational human, law-abiding gods, but vague, irrational, mainly malevolent spirit-things, ghosts and bogeys and the like.'' Such spirits were reverenced mainly in the hope that they would go away and not cause trouble.

With a few notable exceptions, such as Aphrodite and Athena, the feminine deities of Homeric mythology came to be characterized by dark, fearsome traits and behavior that bring to mind the later European myth of the witch. But the shift from worship of a goddess containing life and death in equal measure to one in which the dark side obliterates the light was a gradual process—and one that was never fully brought to its conclusion. Goddesses and gods and higher and lower beings possessed of both good and evil continued to appear in Greek and Roman mythology.

Medusa is a stark example. Queen of the Gorgons, she had hair of vipers and a glance that turned men to stone. Yet even she was shown in myth to have the life-giving force inside her. When the warrior Perseus had cut off her head with his sword, the goddess Athena intervened to allow Asclepius, the god of healing, to draw a sampling of Medusa's blood. Asclepius took his supply from both sides of Medusa's body. Blood from the left side he used to slay his

A snake-handling Minoan figurine embodies the Mother Goddess as worshiped on the isle of Crete in about 1600 BC. The goddess was a study in opposites—a symbol of love and fear who gave life and took it away.

enemies; blood from the right side served in his cures and could bring the dead back to life.

Perhaps even more fearsome than Medusa, if such a thing is possible, was the archsorceress Hecate, feared ruler of the underworld. As the mistress of ghosts and specters, she was thought to possess the power to inflict madness by conjuring terrifying visions. And like the witches of later legend, her powers were believed to be most potent at midnight. Stories told of night travelers who encountered her in remote and lonely places, at the same desolate crossroads where the forces of evil are always rumored to lurk. Some people claimed that Hecate stood 100 feet tall and roamed the countryside with a pack of wild hounds. Others pictured her with three heads—one a thick-maned horse, the next a hissing snake, and the last a savage dog. The howling of canines at night was said to mark Hecate's approach—only dogs, it was thought, could see her clearly.

The Romans, who carried over many Greek deities in forming their own complicated mythology, sought to avoid the wrath of Hecate by leaving offerings of honey cakes and chicken hearts on their doorsteps or by depositing gifts at the crossroads where she sometimes appeared. Sacrifices, the traditional means of appeasing divine anger, were regularly offered to Hecate, and the numerous creatures slaughtered in her name included dogs, female lambs, and even infant girls. Throughout the history of the arcane arts, the name of Hecate has been invoked repeatedly in connection with witches and practitioners of black magic.

The fair-haired enchantress Circe, daughter of Helios, the sun god, was another of the more fully drawn witch prototypes in classical mythology. In *The Odyssey,* Homer's chronicle of the warrior Odysseus's ill-fated journey home from the Trojan War, Circe with her magical powers played a critical role. Having been banished to the isle of Aeaea for poisoning her husband, the king of the Sarma-

The devouring hag Lilitu, here rendered in painted terra cotta, was among the most terrible spirits of Sumerian mythology and a model for the Hebrew demon Lilith. Winged and taloned, she searched for men to seduce and children to murder. Medieval witches inherited many of her traits, including her fondness for owls and cats.

How the Witch Got Her Broom

The now familiar image of a witch flitting through the night sky astride a broomstick made its first known appearance in the fifteenth-century illustration reproduced above. It is taken from the manuscript of *Le Champion des Dames,* or "The Champion of Women," by the Swiss writer Martin Le Franc. But the magical connotations of brooms are far older than the drawing. Brooms have long been associated with female magic and powerful women. At some point, they became the woman's equivalent of the magical staff, such as that used by Moses to part the Red Sea.

Sacred midwives of ancient Rome used brooms to sweep the thresholds of homes where they delivered babies. They believed the sweeping would drive evil spirits from the mothers and infants within. Ever since then, brooms have carried symbolic power in matters mundane and grand. Until quite recently, women in parts of England left their brooms outside their cottages to signal they were out. Some scholars surmise that the idea behind this practice was to leave behind a symbol of the homemaker to safeguard the house. In Wales and among gypsies, marriages were traditionally made complete when the newlyweds leaped over a broomstick upon entering their new home. (Modern witch couples leap over a broom as part of the Wiccan marriage ceremony called handfasting.)

As a symbol with a pagan past, the broom may have aroused particular enmity among the Christian witch hunters. But contrary to popular belief, few of the forced confessions of the witch tribunals alluded to brooms. An exception was the 1598 report of a girl, Claudine Boban, who divulged that "both she and her mother mounted on a besom"—a broom made of twigs—"and that flying out by the chimney they were thus borne through the air to the Sabbat." Although prosecutors sometimes put ideas in their victims' heads, the flying-broom image was not widely adopted for the trials. Nonetheless, the concept took root and is now inseparable from the icon of the witch.

tians, Circe passed her days singing and weaving in a splendid marble palace that was surrounded by lush woods.

When Odysseus landed on the island, he sent out a party to reconnoiter in the command of his trusted friend Eurylochus. As the scouts marched inland, the sweet sound of Circe's singing soon drew them toward her marble palace. Along the way the voyagers were surrounded by a rather daunting assortment of lions, tigers, and wolves that had slipped silently out of the woods. Eurylochus's men were quite naturally alarmed but were relieved to discover that the beasts were of an unusually gentle nature. Unknown to Eurylochus, the animals were in fact a group of former sailors, not unlike themselves, who had been ensnared by Circe and transformed by her magic. With these man-beasts tagging at their heels, Eurylochus and his men drew close to the palace and were immediately beguiled by the music within. Soon Circe appeared and conducted them inside to partake of a great feast. With most of the party eagerly following her lead, only Eurylochus balked, somehow sensing a trap.

nside the palace, Circe seated her guests and served them a meal of cheese, barley, and honeyed wine. All ate heartily, unaware that the sorceress had added to the wine her own "vile pinch," a powerful drug. No sooner had the men drunk this potion than they were rendered helpless, unable to resist the magic of their hostess. Moving about the feasting table, Circe touched each man with a wand, and immediately the sailor was transformed into a hog. Her work complete, Circe shut her new captives in pigsties, with a supply of acorns and other coarse foods.

Having witnessed the misfortune of his fellow crewmen, Eurylochus hurried back to the ship to report the strange tale to Odysseus. Only through the use of a magic herb—a sprig of the legendary plant called moly—was the great warrior able to avoid the same treachery that had befallen his crew. When Circe discovered that her spells held no power over Odysseus, she agreed to release his men from their enchantment. In time, the sorceress grew enamored of Odysseus and eventually gave him the assistance he needed to complete his journey home.

The legend of Circe's niece Medea follows a similar path but comes to a far less happy resolution. In the end, Medea emerged as the very incarnation of the evil witch, bringing havoc and revenge to all who dared to cross her.

Medea was the daughter of the king of Colchis, but she came to loggerheads with her father when she fell in love with Jason, another well-known traveler and adventurer. Captain of the ship *Argo* and leader of its crew, the Argonauts, Jason was near the end of a long and difficult quest to capture the golden fleece, a fabled treasure that had been stolen from the winged ram of the god Hermes and avidly sought ever since its disappearance. Medea's devotion would prove invaluable to Jason, because her father had set a series of seemingly impossible tasks for anyone who hoped to take possession of the golden fleece. In order to claim the prize, Jason would first have to yoke two fire-breathing bulls and put the beasts to work plowing a large field. This done, he would be required to sow a handful of magic dragon's teeth in the furrows and slay whatever enemy appeared as a result. Should Jason survive these tests, he would be permitted to retrieve the golden fleece—but only if he could snatch it from beneath the watchful gaze of a fearsome dragon.

When Jason learned that Medea possessed magical powers, he appealed to her for assistance and promised to take her as his bride in return. Medea joyously assented and at once set out to ensure Jason's success. After instructing him in the challenges that awaited him, she mixed a special ointment that contained the blood of Prometheus, the fire bringer, and told Jason to coat his body with the salve and thus render himself invincible for a day.

The next morning, as the king and the citizens of Colchis watched from a nearby hillside, Jason took his place in an open field opposite the fierce-looking bulls that would be his first opponents. Jets of flame burst from the nostrils of the beasts, scorching the grass at their feet. As Jason approached, they rushed forward with a roar, causing the

The dark side of the Mother Goddess came to the fore in the Greek deity Hecate pictured in this Roman wall painting as a winged figure wielding what appears to be a whip. She was queen of the dead, and her assistance was believed essential to malevolent sorcery.

earth to shake beneath their hooves. Emboldened by the power of Medea's potion, Jason met the bulls' charge with calm assurance and wrestled the bellowing creatures to the ground. His companions cheered with joy when their leader succeeded in slipping the yoke over the heads of the animals. And with the stunned king looking on, Jason proceeded to plow the field of battle in accordance with the instructions he had been given.

His first task acquitted, Jason wasted no time in sprinkling the dragon's teeth into the furrows he had dug. From each tooth sprang a fearsome soldier brandishing weapons and moving forward to press the attack. For a time, Jason was able to hold this phantom army at bay, slashing with his sword and shield. Soon, however, the hero was on the verge of being overwhelmed by the mass of onrushing enemy troops. Once again, Medea's sorcery snatched Jason

from certain destruction. Following the witch's instructions, he hurled a large stone into the midst of his foes. Suddenly, the soldiers turned their weapons on one another, hacking and slashing with a mad fury. In a matter of moments, Jason stood alone in a field littered with corpses.

To claim the golden fleece, Jason still would have to survive an encounter with the dragon that guarded the oak bough where the treasure lay. Cautiously, the warrior crept forward, removing from his belt another potion supplied by Medea. He sprinkled a few drops of this brew on the dragon, and at once the creature, which had never before relaxed its guard for so much as a moment, turned on its side and fell into a heavy slumber. Stealing past the sleeping monster, Jason seized the glittering prize and made his escape, to the surprise and outrage of the king. With Medea in tow, Jason hurried aboard the *Argo* and immediately set sail.

The lovely Circe of Homeric legend used potions to turn men into docile animals. By the time this picture was painted in sixteenth-century Italy, such powers branded their possessor a witch in league with the devil.

Although he had secured the golden fleece, Jason's perils were not yet ended, and it was in the retreat from her father's kingdom that Medea revealed the full horror of her witchy nature. When the king sent an armada in pursuit of the *Argo*, Medea lured her own brother aboard the ship and cast a spell over him. As the young man fell under her thrall, Medea coldly murdered him and sliced his body into pieces. After that, each time the king's ships began to close in on the *Argo*, Medea hurled into the sea a limb from her brother's body, forcing her grief-stricken father to halt his progress and retrieve the pieces for burial. With the assistance of this diversionary action, Jason eventually made good his escape.

Classical mythological figures such as Medea, Hecate, and Medusa no longer much resembled the mother goddesses of earlier cultures, but they retained the two-sided good-and-evil nature that had always been a hallmark of the female deity. The Romans and Greeks also worshiped goddesses closer to the original mold, and some of the rites celebrated in honor of these deities bear resemblance to the later notion of the witches' sabbat. In Rome, a temple was built on the Palatine hill in 204 BC for the mother goddess Cybele.

Medea, a legendary Greek sorceress whose image presaged that of later European witches, draws a rejuvenated ram from her cauldron to demonstrate a magical brew to Aeson, aged father of her husband, Jason. Medea made Aeson young with her sorcery.

Natives of the ancient kingdom of Phrygia were brought to Rome to act as her priests. Although they were males, they dressed as women, wore their hair long, and paid worship to the goddess through orgiastic dances, which they carried on until they dropped in exhaustion. Some scholars believe that the priests of Cybele proved their dedication through self-emasculation.

Similar forms of worship took place in Greece—most notably, in the rites of Dionysus. More typical, however, were the dignified Eleusinian mysteries, which were celebrated in honor of the earth goddess Demeter, wife of Zeus, the king of gods. Demeter's rites followed a traditional pattern that observed the natural cycle of death and rebirth in connection with the growing season.

Of all the deities in classical mythology, the moon goddess called Diana by the Romans and Artemis by the Greeks would be most closely associated with witchcraft.

Artemis-Diana was the patron of both fertility and chastity, and she was also mistress of the hunt. She traveled alone, and for her, the chase was the thing; she seldom engaged in wholesale slaughter. Yet she, too, had her dark side. Beautiful but cold, she was known to turn would-be suitors into game. A hunter called Actaeon chanced to see her bathing nude in a woodland spring one day. To punish him for watching her, she transformed him into a stag, then set his own hounds on him. The hounds were in the process of tearing Actaeon apart when his hunting partners finished him off with their arrows.

Diana also had the power to change her own nature and shape. In some manifestations she was identified with the fearsome three-headed Hecate, and in this form her consorts were vicious owl-like creatures that were known as *strigae*, with huge heads and beaks, grasping talons, and abominable appetites. Strigae flew through the night sky in search of unattended babies, and when they found one, they would rip open its belly and gorge on its entrails. When morning came, it was said, the strigae would assume the shape of apparently harmless old women.

Tales of strigae seem to have originated among the early Germanic peoples of northern Europe and were well established in the Rome of Jesus' time. The poet Ovid described how to hold the child-devouring demons at bay by touching the lintels and threshold of a baby's room with a sprig of arbutus, while placing a wand of whitethorn at the window. Most important of all, advised Ovid, it was necessary to offer the ravenous witch-birds a substitute for the baby, such as the entrails of a suckling pig, saying: "Birds of night, spare this child's vitals! A young victim dies instead of this little baby."

Some years later, the Roman lexicographer Festus, in his work on the meaning of words, formally defined strigae as "women who practice sorcery, and who are called flying women." But Roman law took no notice of such creatures, and nobody was ever arrested for being a witch-bird.

What did concern the ruling elite—and had since the institution of Roman law—was the distinction between

Dancers depicted on a Grecian urn whirl to the music of pipe and cymbals in a
festival honoring Dionysus, the god of wine and fertility. Most of the nocturnal revelers were women,
led by a male priest. With wine drinking, ecstatic dancing, and animal sacrifices,
the Dionysian rites were virtual dress rehearsals for the alleged sabbats of medieval witches.

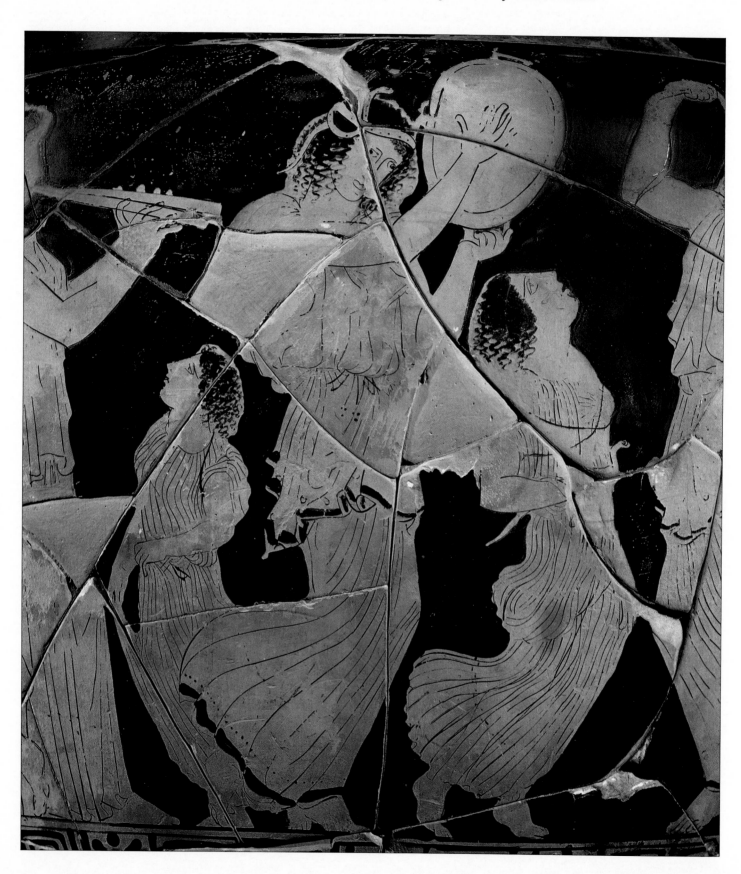

white magic and black. Highborn Romans considered the former acceptable; the latter, they punished in the same manner as any other civic offense that involved harm to person or property. There was an important exception: Any act of apparent sorcery that seemed to threaten the Roman state or the well-being of the emperor met with swift and vigorous reprisal. One unfortunate young man was observed gesturing oddly and reciting Greek vowels at a public bath. He was merely trying to cure a stomach cramp, but the authorities feared he might be casting a spell against the emperor. Summarily arrested, he was tortured and put to death. The harsh treatment of malevolent magic in Roman law probably did much to lay the groundwork for the prosecution of alleged witches in medieval Europe. But wholesale roundups and burnings of witches were still more than a millennium in the future.

Up until the collapse of the Roman Empire, to be called a witch in Europe usually meant nothing more than to be called a practitioner of sorcery—a relatively commonplace activity. Sorcerers were sprinkled throughout most communities; they cultivated magical powers that they hoped would enable them to attain practical ends, such as fertilizing their fields or punishing their enemies.

Although they may at times have sought to exploit evil spirits in pursuit of such goals, there is little indication that they actually venerated demons, as the Catholic church would later contend. A burial site unearthed in northern Europe showed that the practice of sorcery on the Continent dates from a very early time—as seems to be the case in every part of the world. A grave held the skeleton of a Bronze Age sorceress surrounded by the tools of her trade: the bones of a weasel, the claw joint of a lynx, snake vertebrae, horses' teeth, a broken knife blade, and some bits of fool's gold. What magical properties these artifacts possessed and what wonders the sorceress worked can only be imagined.

Later history records that sorcerers brewed potions to inspire love, offered charms and amulets to protect against injury, and used their magical skills to cure disease. One Anglo-Saxon recipe for the treatment of warts called for "the water of a dog and the blood of a mouse" to be mixed together and smeared on the afflicted part. Sorcerers among these same people concocted a "pleasant drink against insanity" from catnip, wormwood, lupine, radish, fennel, cat's mint, enchanter's nightshade, and a number of other herbs all steeped in strong ale. This formula, dating from the Christian era, included a dose of that religion. "Sing twelve Masses over the drink, and let the patient drink it. He will soon be better," advised the sorcerer.

From earliest times, it was well known that every sorcerer possessed two sides, a light and a dark, benign and evil—like so many of the sorceresses of myth. The northern peoples turned to sorcery to improve their position at the expense of their neighbors or simply to vent their spleen. The ancient Teutonic tribes, to avenge some real or imagined wrong, would fashion images of their enemies in dough or wax. These they would plunge into water or stab with needles or toss into the fire, in hopes of drowning or maiming or roasting the individuals portrayed. And the Anglo-Saxons dealt with their opponents by reciting a spell that shrank the offender by degrees until he was no larger than "the hip bone of an itch mite."

Because of this dual capacity for good and evil, every practitioner of magic and sorcery, no matter how closely attached to a tribe or family, was regarded with grave uneasiness. The folktales of the Celtic and Germanic peoples reflect a deep-seated fear of the sorcerer's presumed mastery over the most frightful powers of nature. They show that long before people made the connection between human magic and the powers of Satan, they believed that sorcerers could command the storm clouds, cause harvests to wither and die, unleash famine, and bring down pestilence. No one was considered immune to the sorcerer's spell. An angry magician could influence the process of life itself, making men impotent and inducing entire herds of cattle to abort their calves.

The Germanic goddess Holda rides the wind with spirits of the dead in this nineteenth-century painting. On her Wild Hunt, Holda was believed to sweep over the countryside, rewarding and punishing peasants for their care of the land. In time, her rampaging horde came to be identified with the witches thought to roam medieval forests.

Secretive by nature, the strange spirit-beings thought to hold such powers were believed to be most at home in the night, riding out on the backs of wolves or wild boars or on fence posts, to rendezvous with deities of earth and sky. An old Norse tale recounts the astonishment of its hero when he was roused from sleep by a great uproar in the forest and rushed out to find "a sorceress with streaming hair" bound for a "magic meeting" with Skelking, the Scandinavian sky lord.

Such midnight spirit revels were part of every European folklore, and they closely foreshadowed later Christian descriptions of witches meeting with Satan. In northern lands, gatherings of sorcerers were conducted by the goddess Holda, wife of Wotan, whose sphere of patronage included farming, childbirth, marriage, and the home. Holda's name and nature varied from one region to another. Some people called her Holle or Frau Hoff or identified her with the great goddess Freyja; to others she was Bertha or Perchta, goddess of the hunt. Holda was the Germanic counterpart to the moon goddess Diana, who was worshiped in the lands to the south.

Holda's train of followers might include Valkyries, the female sky warriors of Nordic lore, or the souls of dead children, or various demonic characters who were known by the euphemism "good ladies of the night." She was most active in the cold months, particularly during the winter solstice, when her nocturnal jaunts were thought to revive the sun and ensure good harvests for the coming year. When she made her bed, the feathers fell to earth in the form of snowflakes, bringing fertility to the soil. More often than not she was a motherly, protective goddess—although when Holda was roused to anger, she could be transformed into an ugly old hag with buck teeth and a long pointy nose, the terror of unruly children.

The goddess of fertility could thus become the queen of mayhem, and in some traditions her midnight revels were seen as destructive routs. On such a *Wilde Jagd,* or Wild Hunt, gangs of demonic savages, half human and half animal, would ravage the countryside, plundering and murdering, and devouring the bodies of their victims. Masculine spirits also rode out on the Wilde Jagd. Herne the Hunter, a Celtic deity with antlers sprouting from his forehead, was believed to lead a band of lecherous, satyrlike creatures on similar rampages in Britain.

Holda's equivalent in the regions now referred to as Scandinavia was the great goddess Freyja, who belonged to a group of deities known as the Vanir. Primarily associated with fertility, the Vanir brought to humanity the power to create new life—whether in the fields, among animals, or in the home. In addition, they served as a link to the unseen world through their wondrous powers of divination, foretelling the coming seasons and the fortunes of men. However, like Holda and so many of the Greek goddesses, they too possessed a terrible capacity for violence. Their deeds inspired a cult of worshipers whose rites included wild, orgiastic revels and sacrificial ceremonies similar to those later attributed to witch covens.

As priestess of the Vanir, Freyja was sometimes called the possessor of the slain. Her duties included assigning seats in heaven to half of the heroes killed in battle—the other half were attended to by Odin, the supreme god of the Norse world. Like the mythical beings of the Greek and Roman worlds, Freyja could change forms, and Norse tales describe how she would soar through the heavens in the body of a bird or else thunder about in a chariot drawn by cats. A legendary beauty and utterly promiscuous, the goddess was an object of desire among the giants who lived in the fabled realm of Jotunheim.

Seior, the ritual witchcraft that folklore described as the key to Freyja's powers of prophecy, developed a particularly dark strain as it was passed down among her worshipers. Folk sorcerers among the Norsemen would attempt to inflict evil upon an enemy by planting a horse's head, mouth agape, in front of his abode. One seiokona—a practitioner of seior—allegedly took the form of a horse and then attacked a king and crushed him to death. In Iceland, a woman accused of practicing seior was brought to trial for having "ridden a man to death."

Portrayed on a cauldron, the antlered Celtic god Cernunnos is surrounded by animals real and imaginary. Belief in Cernunnos pervaded northern Europe in the pre-Christian era, possibly because he was thought to hold power over fertility and wealth. His popularity made him a target for the Church, which saw horns as a feature of the devil.

In one divination rite known as the *seidr*, a seeress called a *völva* would ascend a high platform and sing spells to put herself in a trance. While she was in this condition, the seeress would seek information from the spirit world that would enable her to answer questions put to her by fellow worshipers. Such a rite did not serve any purpose in solitude, so the völva would travel among the people, visiting farms and attending feasts as a means of dispensing advice for the coming seasons.

One account of a seidr describes a village in Greenland that had been sorely afflicted by famine. The local townspeople awaited the predictions of their itinerant seeress with great interest and considerable anxiety. To ensure the prophecy's success, they prepared a lavish sacrificial meal that included the hearts of every different animal they could obtain. Once this feast had been consumed, the völva

28

that she said," recorded one observer, "went unfulfilled."

Because of the open, communal nature of the seidr, it was in one important regard quite different from the fabled nighttime meetings of witches. But even such public comings together for purposes of creating magic undoubtedly contributed to the folklore of the sabbat.

Like the early Germanic and Nordic peoples, the Celtic race had its own traditions of powerful female deities, whose characteristics echoed what was by that time the all-but-forgotten memory of the ancient mother goddesses. For the most part, the rituals of the Celts in observance of their goddesses were peaceable: They marked the passing of the seasons and gave people a way to seek supernatural protection for their cattle and crops. The goddesses of Celtic mythology, however, also played a substantial role in governing the fortunes of war. In legends, they instructed the local warriors in the arts of battle and employed their magic to the advantage of the Celtic armies. And these deities co-existed, in the rich folklore of the British Isles, with an extraordinary variety of demons, nymphs, and sprites. Among this fanciful cast of spirits were some of the most fully drawn and evocative precursors of the modern stereotype of the witch as an evil hag.

One story containing such a figure is the tale of Niall, the son of Eochu Muigmedon, an early king of Ireland. While Niall and his four brothers were hunting one day, according to this legend, they grew thirsty and sought relief at a well. As they approached the watering hole, a horrendous old crone stepped from her place of concealment. "She was as black as coal," the account reveals. "Her hair was like a wild horse's tail. Her foul teeth were visible from ear to ear and were such as would sever a branch of green oak. Her eyes were black, her nose crooked and spread. Her body was scrawny, spotted and diseased. Her shins were bent. Her knees and ankles were thick, her shoulders broad, her nails were green."

In return for a drink of water from the well, this repulsive figure demanded a kiss from each of the princes in

mounted her traditional high platform wearing boots of calfskin and gloves sewn together from the hide of a cat and was seated on a cushion filled with hen feathers. When she asked for a villager to come forward to sing the incantation that would put her in a receptive state of mind, a young Christian woman volunteered, claiming to have learned the song as a girl.

As this woman began to sing, the völva fell at once into a deep trance in which she lingered for quite some time. When at last she regained normal consciousness, she informed the assembly that the singing had been so successful that spirits had thronged to hear it. From them, the seeress said, she had learned that the famine would end before long. She made various other predictions as well—foretelling, among other things, the destiny of the woman whose singing had produced the successful trance. "Little

turn. The brothers were understandably reluctant to grant her request, and only Niall, who perhaps sensed that magic was afoot, stepped forward and cautiously offered the required kiss. Like the frog-princes of later folklore, the misshapen hag was at once transformed into a young woman of stunning beauty.

In the milieu of magical belief and practice that spawned such fairy tales, the Celts were not about to forgo the benefits of sorcery in marking their most significant occasions, such as the inauguration of kings. The process of selecting Celtic monarchs at one time included a bizarre fertility rite—the ceremonial mating of the intended ruler with the local goddess in the form of a pure white mare. As late as the twelfth century, this rather barbarous practice was still performed. After one such ritual, according to a contemporary chronicle, the mare was immediately killed, hacked into pieces, and boiled in a large cauldron. The chosen ruler then lowered himself into the broth and dined on horse flesh as he bathed. Tradition required him to drink the broth not with a cup or even with his hand but by lapping it up in the manner of a beast. "These unrighteous things being duly accomplished," the account concludes, "his royal authority and dominion are ratified."

ith a magical world view thus woven into the fabric of society, from top to bottom, it is not likely that the Celts would have looked upon sorcery as a threat to society. They did not, but neither did they allow maleficium to go unpunished. Harm done to an individual by occult means was treated as a crime against that particular person and his or her kin. In England, murderers suspected of having employed sorcery were turned over to the family of the victim for punishment.

The legal treatment of sorcery was similar throughout most of Europe, particularly in the Germanic lands, where the custom was to allow victims of maleficium to seek private retribution. As related in the tenth-century Icelandic saga, *Eyrbyggia,* a widow, whose incantations were thought to have made a young man gravely ill, was hunted down and stoned to death by his kinsmen. Another saga of the period, *Laxdaela,* describes how a married couple, both sorcerers, brought about the death of a twelve-year-old boy by magical incantations. Again, the victim's family caught the criminals and stoned them to death. However, as early as AD 500, the Salian Franks in what is now France had settled for more lenient penalties. "If a witch shall devour a man and it be proved against her," decreed the *Lex Salica,* she must pay his family a fine equivalent to 200 gold shillings, with a lesser sum if she simply made her victim sick. A death penalty, usually by burning, could be exacted only if the witch pleaded guilty or if she was a serf and could not muster the gold to pay her fine.

At the same time, Salic law discouraged people from making idle accusations against innocent neighbors. An equally stiff fine was exacted from anyone who was rash enough to call a person a witch and was not able to prove it. In such cases, the accuser also was required to pay the costs of the trial. The Lombards of northern Italy likewise warned against such slander: "Let nobody presume to kill a foreign serving-maid or female slave as a *striga,* for such a thing is not possible," their code admonished, "nor ought it to be at all believed by Christian minds that a woman can eat up a living man from within."

Sadly, such moderate and confident attitudes never seemed to persist for long. A magical world view was too powerful in Europe, among pagans and Christians alike. The messages of mythology and folklore were not buried deep in the human psyche; they held real and immediate meaning. They also communicated a delicate balance of love and hate for the sorceress, a figure of seemingly enormous power. And that balance, it seems, was always ready to tip in the direction of fear and dread. People thought that they knew what a witch was; in fact, they knew her by a dozen different names. All they needed was one more reason to give in to their instincts to strike out against this source of uncertainty. Unfortunately, that is exactly what they got as Christianity asserted its claims to both their lives and their loyalty.

Throughout history, people who could unlock nature's botanical secrets, who knew which plants could kill, cure, or distort reality, were regarded with awe and fear. Monks and physicians were among those privy to the hidden powers of berries, blossoms, leaves, and roots. Witches, however, were believed to surpass all others in the scope of their herbal magic.

Many who were rumored to be witches, or were persecuted as such, were probably skilled herbalists. And much of the lore regarding their powers was a blend of fiction and fact. By combining the right mix of herbs, it was thought, witches could fly through the air, strike down enemies, blight cattle and crops, or enamor a hapless suitor. But when the mood struck them, they could use their powers constructively. They could heal, for instance, by administering foxglove *(above)* to someone with an ailing heart.

Herbal magic was said to function in various ways. Some worked through vapors. A crop-killing storm, say, might be summoned by the fumes of certain noxious plants boiled up with venomous snakes and black roosters. Love elixirs, on the other hand, required ingestion, and "flying ointments," which contained herbs that modern scientists have found produce hallucinatory sensations of flight, were applied to the skin.

A number of herbs said to help a witch soar through the air are shown on the next two pages; botanical ingredients favored for love potions and other magic purposes, some plants with real healing properties, and some plants used as antidotes to magic spells appear on the pages that follow.

The thorn apple's prickles warned all but witches away from its poisonous berries. A few drops of hallucinogenic toxins from the fruit, mixed into a flying ointment, reportedly caused hours of visions.

Monkshood's lovely clusters of purple cowl-shaped flowers belie the plant toxicity. Sacred to Hecate, the patron of witches and queen of the underworld in Greek mythology, monkshood disturbs the rhythms of the heart, thereby producing a feeling of falling or flying.

The inky juice of deadly nightshade's gleaming berries rubbed on the skin created vertiginous tremors that may have contributed to the sensation of flight. Better known as belladonna, the plant can also cause distorted vision, which might have made a witch's illusion of flying all the more real.

White water lily was another of the many plants and flowers said to play a part in flying ointments. Such additives as toad's venom, donkey's lung, tomb dust, and even the fat of unbaptized babies rounded out the common recipes of legend.

Within the lace-topped stalks of the hemlock plant is a deadly nectar that was believed to enhance the sense of gliding through the air. To speed up the effects of the flying ointment, a witch would spread it over areas of her body where the skin was most thin and sensitive. Rumor held that she applied the ointment to her genital membranes.

Although the cinquefoil lacks any chemical properties that would add to the pharmacological effects of a flying ointment, some herbalists associated its five-fingered leaves with the five senses of the body. As a result, flying ointments may have been heavily laden with cinquefoil leaves, in hopes of intensifying the sensual experience of soaring.

Spellbinding Plants

Witches relied on the opium poppy (right) for its passion-inhibiting properties. Its narcotic juices neatly dispatched an amorous man into a deep, forgetful sleep.

Once called sorcerer's violet, periwinkle (below) was allegedly powdered with earthworms and served with meat to ignite sparks between a man and a woman.

The poisonous Christmas rose was believed to serve in numerous powerful spells, including one that could ensure invisibility: A witch simply sprinkled pieces of the plant before her and vanished.

Witches reputedly used twigs of the witch hazel, a North American shrub (right), as divining rods to find hidden riches. The plant drew its name from this supposed application and the unrelated British hazel shrub.

The much-fabled mandrake was the prize of the witch's pharmacopoeia and figured into most spells of a sexual nature. Its green berries, sometimes called love apples, energized charms designed to arouse passion or produce pregnancy. Its gnarled root, manlike in form, figured in potions to restore virility.

Another standby in love elixirs, endive (right) derives its aphrodisiac connotations from a druidic myth in which a girl spurns the advances of the sun god. The angry deity transforms her into endive, thus forcing her to gaze upon him each day.

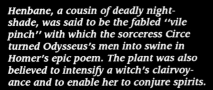

Henbane, a cousin of deadly nightshade, was said to be the fabled "vile pinch" with which the sorceress Circe turned Odysseus's men into swine in Homer's epic poem. The plant was also believed to intensify a witch's clairvoyance and to enable her to conjure spirits.

Long a symbol of female creative power, the rose (above) was conscripted into the service of the witch, who distilled its beauty into a potion designed to entice the wavering or reluctant suitor.

Healing Herbs

While the purple-belled fox-glove is lethal when ingested in quantity, the sorceress who used it with a light hand found that it helped control heart disease. Physicians borrowed this wisdom and today prescribe a foxglove derivative, digitalis, for cardiac conditions.

A staple in the witch's botanical pharmacy was the dainty weed ground ivy. The plant was used to relieve constricted tissue in cases of muscle cramps or asthma.

The herb vervain was best known as a pain-killer. The analgesic had special value for witches—it would allegedly harden the body against the agonies of torture and fire.

From ergot, a fungus that grows
on ryegrass—shown at right
blackening the rye grains—the
herbalists concocted a drug
designed to help women manage the pains of labor and
delivery. Ergot-based drugs are
still used in childbirth today.

The well-prepared witch may
have taken a dose of smallage,
or wild celery (above), before a
night's flight; the root was believed to prevent muscle cramps.

Brews containing parsley leaves
were once believed to induce
abortion. Some medieval women,
weakened by frequent childbear-
ing and shunned by the village
doctor, secretly visited the local
witch in order to unburden themselves of unwanted pregnancies.

Plants for Protection

During the medieval era, the witch provided a convenient scapegoat for all that was deemed evil or that was not fully understood. Villagers angered or frightened by the apparent power of sorcery attempted to fight fire with fire by mustering herbal magic of their own. In the process, a guardian tree or flower was identified to protect against almost every form of misfortune, illness, or tragedy.

These pages depict an assortment of plants deemed crucial in fending off witchcraft. Some served prophylactically, providing a defense against potential mischief, whereas others acted as antidotes for evil already inflicted.

Angelica, with its chaste snowball flowers, was revered as the "holy plant," the strongest known deterrent to witchcraft. Legend credits the discovery of its powers to a monk, which may explain the flower's religious connotations.

The yellow-flowered mullein stalk (below) was dipped in suet to create a hag's taper, a candle said to repel witches. In Italy, the plant was called light of the Lord since it foiled the works of the devil.

Parents protected their offspring against witch's spells by sewing sprigs of red rowan berries (above) into the children's clothing. Farmers sought to prevent their cattle from being bewitched by tying small crosses made from rowan branches beneath the tails of the animals.

Delicate betony flowers (left) were so effective in guarding against witches' spells that an old adage advised, ''Sell your coat, and buy betony.''

Dill's greenish yellow blooms (below) were thought extremely repugnant to the witch and were used to drive her away.

A dose of the wholesome flower mallow (above) sometimes fortified a village physician's prescriptions; it was considered an antidote to many of the ailments wrought by witchcraft.

Travelers carried sprays of the shrub mugwort (left) when embarking upon a journey. The plant was reputed to shield one from the powers of the evil eye.

CHAPTER 2

The Horror of the Witch Hunt

ne day early in the ninth century, no less a personage than the bishop of Lyons, a thoughtful man named Agobard, chanced upon an angry mob of peasants as he made his way through the French countryside. The noisy crowd was roughly manhandling four strangers—a woman and three men. Some of the countryfolk were gathering up rocks, clearly intending to stone their captives to death. At the approach of the prelate the commotion abated; peasant men doffed their caps.

What was afoot, the bishop inquired. Who were these unfortunates and what was their offense that they should be seized and threatened so? Why, they were *tempestarii,* a peasant explained—storm makers. They had fallen out of their cloud ship and into the hands of the villagers before they could accomplish their foul magical deeds, thank God. And now the peasants were about to ensure that these four witches never destroyed another crop. As Bishop Agobard noted in a passage of his voluminous writings, in those days most people of all ranks believed in tempestarii, who were thought to conjure up violent storms through sorcery. Under cover of the tempests, it was said, they used their magic to steal crops, which they loaded into their cloud ships and carried off, planning to market them in a fabled country called Mangonia.

In fact, not all tempestarii were imaginary, although their supposed powers may have been. For centuries before Bishop Agobard's time—and for centuries after—self-proclaimed storm makers traveled about Europe reportedly calling up nasty bouts of winds, rain, hail, and lightning by the simple act of churning and beating the waters of a pond or, if no pond was available, making a puddle of urine and stirring it with a finger. But usually they did not have to demonstrate their powers, because the mere threat of a harvest-ruining storm intimidated peasant farmers into paying the tempestarii to make their magical turbulence elsewhere, over someone else's fields. In the lands ruled by Visigoths during the sixth century, this kind of extortion had been common enough to warrant a standard penalty for storm makers: 200 lashes and the ignominy of being paraded with shorn heads through the neighborhood villages.

Whether the four people Agobard found in jeopardy were working that medieval protection racket, or whether they were innocent victims of mistaken identity, is not known. In any case—and this is the significance of the tale—the bishop rescued them from the furious mob.

This was a time when belief in *maleficium,* the doing of harm by occult means, was a fact of everyday life. The average man was convinced that a deserted mistress who knew sorcery could take her revenge if he married another. The wronged woman had only to tie three knots in a string during his wedding; the knots would make him impotent. A herder could mutter a spell over a hunk of bread and conceal it in a tree to direct disease and injury away from his livestock and toward a neighbor's. If a beekeeper knew the right charms to use, she could attract to her hives all the honey in the district, or so it was said. And a person thoroughly versed in witching powers supposedly could achieve even worse maleficium—could make a wax puppet, say, and drive nails into it to murder an enemy.

Alleged acts of maleficium might stir public anger, as the scene Agobard encountered indicates. Documents of the era chronicle a number of incidents involving lynch mobs that seized suspected witches and beat them, dunked them repeatedly, or burned them at the stake. But although the people dealt out their own rough justice now and again, more alleged witches were tolerated than attacked, especially those who were thought capable of healing ailing neighbors or helping fellow villagers fend off evil. Moreover, neither church nor secular authorities expended much energy in the pursuit of witches in those days. Despite the fact that many forms of maleficium violated ecclesiastical or civil law, there were very few prosecutions for such offenses before the fourteenth century. Indeed, clergymen themselves were rumored to dabble in sorcery, at least in the higher-level occult practices that were known as ritual magic; and since clerics were among the few who could read the old magic books, such suspicions were understandable. And that a prominent bishop, a pillar of the Church, would interrupt his business to save the lives of four suspected storm makers—such reasonableness was indeed a remarkable contrast to what the future would bring.

For Europe's attitude toward witchcraft was changing, and the time would come when any Roman Catholic bishop, far from going out of his way to rescue alleged witches, would more likely be sending scores of them to their deaths. Commencing in the fourteenth century, the Continent was to witness a frenzy of hatred and homicidal witch-baiting that would cost the lives of many thousands of innocent people over the next 300 years. Like brush fires spread by wind-borne sparks, the fury would erupt first in one place, then in another, searing the civilized life of France, Italy, Germany, the Low Countries, Spain, England, Scotland, Austria, Norway, Finland, and Sweden, and for one brief period, leaping the Atlantic to flare up even in the New World.

When the witch hunt struck a community, its horrors came to pervade almost every aspect of existence. No one was safe: not the rich, certainly not the poor, neither the young nor the old. Even the magistrates themselves were sometimes accused and convicted of the very crimes they ascribed to those who appeared before them. Torture and fear twisted truth into grotesque, unrecognizable travesties and shattered traditional loyalties like a sledgehammer smashing a clay pot. Neighbors accused one another, God-fearing Christians pointed at their fellow worshipers, children testified against their parents.

In countless civil trials and the dread tribunals of the Inquisition, accusation was tantamount to conviction, conviction an almost certain sentence of death. Scourged and mutilated by the torturers, flesh torn and bones crushed, the hapless victims confessed to what in retrospect seems a nonsensical mixture of serious and silly charges, from blighting cattle to flying through the air, from murdering babies to kissing the devil's backside. The lucky ones were then beheaded or put to death in some other relatively hu-

mane way before their bodies were reduced to ashes in ovens. But the unlucky ones were burned alive—with green wood to prolong the agony if they had transgressed in some particularly annoying way, such as attempting to recant their confessions.

As the slaughter reached its climax in the domains of Germany in the mid-1600s, whole villages were depopulated at a stroke. According to some perhaps exaggerated accounts, the chief witchcraft prosecutor of Saxony, one Benedict Carpzov, personally signed no fewer than 20,000 death warrants. Many of the court documents have been lost, however, and the full number of judicial murders will never really be known. The best estimate is that possibly 200,000 people were condemned to death as witches before the mania with its mass trials ran its course in the closing decades of the seventeenth century. All in all it was a dark, ugly, and shameful experience for Western civilization and for Christianity.

The Church was primarily responsible for the change in public attitude and official policy that led to the great witch hunt. After the fall of the Roman Empire, the Church had been the only institution strong enough to maintain a kind of order and universality of culture in western Europe. Even as the power of Rome had declined, Christian missionaries such as Saint Patrick and Saint Benedict had traveled throughout the empire and beyond, spreading the gospel to Roman colonists and so-called barbarians alike. The missionaries founded monasteries where dedicated scholars could withdraw from the world's turbulence to keep alive the flickering light of learning. In Rome itself, the papacy actually grew stronger as secular authority waned. Hence, by the time the city's Germanic conquerors marched through Trajan's imperial arch, many of their leaders had already been Christianized.

As time wore on, the influence of the Church became all-encompassing. Yet large numbers of nominal Christians in northern Europe still clung to certain pagan beliefs of their forebears. Particularly troublesome to Church authori-

frenzy and on occasion engage in sexual orgies reminiscent of the Roman Saturnalia and the Dionysian revels of ancient Greece.

Although the Church might have deplored such festivities, it could not entirely suppress them, so it resorted to a shrewd expedient. The pagan feast days were incorporated into the Church calendar. For example, the Roman Saturnalia became Christmas Eve. The great Celtic festival of the dead, Samhain, which marked the beginning of winter and the Celtic new year, fell on October 31. In order to draw attention away from Samhain, the Church declared November 1 to be All Saints' Day, with masses sung to honor departed holy men and women.

But the Church's attempt to assimilate the old festivals was not entirely successful. The pre-Christian spirits that had roamed the earth since the dawn of time were too deeply embedded in the European psyche. Even today in some Western countries, people celebrate October 31—known in the Christian calendar as All Hallows' Eve, or Halloween—with activities that recall the ancient Samhain feast of the dead and by wearing costumes representing skeletons, ghosts, and witches. In those days, the tenacity of the old religious ideas was much more evident. As late as the eighth century, a backwoods Christian priest was found offering a sacrifice to Jupiter, and some isolated communities continued to worship trees and fountains. In a further effort to extinguish the pre-Christian loyalties, the Church declared the pagan gods to be demons.

The woodland sprites of northern climes, the elves, gnomes, ogres, and leprechauns, and the fauns and satyrs of the Mediterranean—all were condemned as enemies of the true Church. An act of homage to them was sacrilege, calling forth the gravest consequences. "If anyone sacrifices a human being to the Devil," declared an edict to the Saxons in 787, referring to a savage rite honoring the god Wotan, "and offers sacrifices to demons as is the custom of the pagans, he shall be put to death."

The architect of this decree was the emperor Charlemagne, king of the Franks, defender of the faith, and the

ties were the old fertility rites and other pagan feast days. In virtually every region, from late fall to early spring, there were days of celebration when people would hold feasts honoring Thor, Wotan, and the other gods; light bonfires; and perform various rituals intended to restore vigor to the low-lying sun. In some rites, the celebrants would don animal skins and headdresses, or disguise themselves as women, to join the ranks of the god and goddess Herne and Holda and their spirit retinues. Wine and beer would flow in copious amounts; dancers would work themselves into a most powerful monarch in Christendom—who, interestingly enough, was not himself baptized until he lay on his deathbed. His territories spanned the length and breadth of Europe, from the Pyrenees to the Danube, and at the Church's bidding he felt obliged to stamp out all evidence of paganism within this vast domain. Not only idolatry, but every type of magic and occult malfeasance, was to be sternly dealt with. Another law demanded that sorcerers and fortunetellers be handed over to the Church for punishment or to be used as slaves. The punishments depended on the nature of the crime. A first offender might have his head shaved and be paraded through town on a donkey. For a second offense, he could have his nose and tongue lopped off, and if brought before the judge a third time, the miscreant risked death.

These provisions were not always rigorously enforced, however, and even some high church officials were said to experiment with magic. But the statutes remained law, and Charlemagne's successors would periodically reassert them. Sorcerers in particular were considered a danger to the realm, as a synod of bishops informed the emperor's son, Louis the Pious, in 829: "Their *maleficia* can disturb the air, bring down hail, foretell the future, remove the fruits and milk from one person and give them to another, and perform innumerable marvels." Witches must be routed out and punished, the bishops said, and "all the more severely because their wicked and overweening audacity does not shrink from serving the Devil."

Witches as the devil's servants—a new and sinister connection had been added to the campaign against paganism. The sorceress of ancient times, stirring her cauldron, brewing up an occasional thunderstorm, perhaps riding out under a full moon with Holda and her court, had now become an instrument of ultimate evil, blasphemous and depraved. A friend and agent of demons, the sorceress was God's enemy as well.

The new concept of witchcraft, involving homage to demons, took inspiration from various arcane issues of

At the devil's bidding, a novice witch tramples the cross, symbolically abjuring Christianity. This and the next five woodcuts, from Francesco-Maria Guazzo's 1626 Compendium Maleficarum (Handbook of Witches), show the process of making a pact with the devil.

While other would-be witches watch, the devil sprinkles an initiate with a vile liquid. In Guazzo's words, "the witch is rebaptized in the name of the Devil, and, having renounced his Christian name, takes another." The act supposedly invalidated the Christian baptism.

Christian theology. One question that had troubled the early Church fathers was how to account for the existence of evil: If God was good, and all-powerful, then why did evil persist in the world? Among the many philosophers to address this thorny issue was Saint Augustine of Hippo, the acknowledged mentor of all later theologians. Writing in the fifth century, Augustine declared that when time first began, God had divided creation into two contrasting realms: a City of God, which was inhabited by angels and all good people, and a City of the Devil, where dwelled demons and their pagan worshipers.

The two domains were continually at war, and all history recorded the struggle between them. Demons were the agents of the devil, armies of invisible beings who inhabited the very air everyone breathed and who never ceased their efforts to corrupt the souls of God-fearing Christians. Among their weapons were magic and sorcery, which they employed to seduce innocent people into worshiping them. Even such common practices as wearing amulets, casting horoscopes, and reciting charms to heal the sick must be shunned as demonic aberrations. Thus it seemed only natural that the undesirable folk healers, fortunetellers, and sorcerers should be lumped together, condemned as members of the devil's demonic host.

The idea that a human could enter into a pact with Satan was nothing new. One such tale, first reported in Greek, then translated into Latin, and finally rendered into verse in the 900s, concerned a sixth-century priest named Theophilus. Steward of an important church in Asia Minor, Theophilus was an ambitious cleric who thought he should be made bishop. Instead, thanks to malicious gossip, he was dismissed from office. In response, he angrily turned to a sorcerer, who arranged for a meeting with the devil. At the appointed hour, so went the tale, Satan appeared and offered a written pact. The terms of the contract required that Theophilus renounce Christ and pledge himself to the devil's service, upon which he would be restored to his

The apprentice witches, gathered within a circle on the ground, swear allegiance to the devil. Guazzo thought they stood in the circle because the devil wanted them to believe that "he is lord of heaven and earth, or possibly because the circle is the symbol of divinity."

The devil holds two books before the group of novice witches. At this point in the ceremony, according to Guazzo, who was an Italian friar, "the witches request the Devil that their names be struck out of the book of life and inscribed in the book of death."

former post. The priest signed and was duly reinstated. What followed were years of bitter remorse, in which the cleric began to appreciate the enormity of his sin. Finally, according to the story, the Virgin Mary herself interceded; the contract was torn up, and Theophilus was saved from the clutches of the devil.

The fable became immensely popular in tenth-century Europe and inspired numerous other accounts of Satanic contracts. Did an amorous swain seek the favors of a demure young maiden? Nothing simpler. The young man merely wrote the devil a letter repudiating his baptism, and the maiden fell into his arms. As such stories circulated, they added another feature to the emerging portrait of occult evildoers: Witchcraft meant entering into a formal covenant with the devil, in which one denied Christ and forfeited one's soul to the powers of darkness.

Some Church fathers were having second thoughts about attributing so much power to the devil's disciples, however. A document calculated to counteract this tenden-cy was written by an anonymous priest, probably during the ninth century. The pronouncement was called the *Canon Episcopi* and early in the tenth century was included in a guide for bishops. In sum, it said that witches and other sorcerers did not actually possess the occult abilities that had been credited to them, and that their sin was in *believing* that they did. For instance, the *Canon* addressed the popular belief that witches made airborne nocturnal journeys in the company of spirits. "Some wicked women, turning back to Satan and seduced by the illusions and phantoms of demons," it observed, "believe and openly avow that in the hours of night they ride upon certain beasts, together with Diana, goddess of the pagans, and a numberless multitude of other women."

Such supernatural goings-on simply did not occur, scoffed the document's author. But that so many people could be made to believe that they did constituted fresh evidence of the devil's handiwork; such delusions could only have been put into people's heads by the archfiend himself.

A child lies helpless on the ground between the devil and his followers, symbolizing the young ones they must destroy. "The witches promise sacrifices of little children," Guazzo explained, "killing one by sorcery every month or sucking its blood every fortnight."

In the final step of the pact with Satan, the witches kneel before the enthroned devil and swear to desecrate all symbols of Christianity. According to Guazzo, the new disciples also pledged that they would "maintain the strictest silence about their traffic with the devil."

Theophilus, a Greek priest, honors the devil in this thirteenth-century illustration. According to the sixth-century story, the first to be written about a devil's pact, the defrocked priest was reinstated after agreeing to embrace the demon.

Priests were sternly enjoined to warn their congregations that Satan knew how to deceive ignorant women; he would indoctrinate them with all sorts of evil images while they were sleeping.

Over time the Church gradually reversed this position, and theologians again began to subscribe to the idea that night flights, transformation into animals, and all the rest really did take place. The *Canon Episcopi* was explained away by arguing that while it may have applied to the time in which it was written, a new army of witches had since arisen who could in fact perform all the things demonologists imputed to them.

The devil's business grew ever more depraved. Beyond the traditional forms of misconduct and maleficium, witches displayed the harpylike qualities of the ancient Roman *strigae,* Hecate's mortal-devouring companions. They would slip out at night, leaving their husbands asleep, pass wraithlike through the locked door if need be, and then roam over thousands of miles, killing and eating Christians or else plucking out their hearts and replacing them with nothing but straw.

Nor was that the worst of it, according to the demonologists. Sexually insatiable, a night-riding witch might transform herself into a beautiful phantom known as a suc-

An Endorsement from Demons

Father Urbain Grandier's predilection for young women was not unusual; in seventeenth-century France, worldly priests abounded. But the handsome cleric from Loudun had been perilously indiscreet, allegedly fathering a baby by the local prosecutor's daughter. He also had a politically injudicious tongue, and this explosive mix gained him dangerous enemies. Ultimately, one of the most powerful men in France, Cardinal Richelieu, engineered the priest's downfall by arranging for him to be accused of witchcraft.

Central to the plot were the nuns at the Loudun convent, who were persuaded to act as if they had been bewitched by Father Grandier and possessed by demons. In November 1633, Grandier was arrested. His fate was sealed by two letters the prosecution produced at his trial. The first *(below, left)*, allegedly penned by the priest, swore allegiance to the devil. The second *(below, right)* accepted the pledge and was witnessed by demons; the Latin words were written backward and from right to left, reputedly to show the devil's contempt for Christianity. Although the letters were clearly faked and some nuns tried to recant their statements, the court found Grandier guilty of witchcraft. He was burned alive in August 1634.

cubus in order to have unholy intercourse with sleeping men. And waking ones as well. One story, transcribed in England in the twelfth century, relates how a roisterous knight named Edric the Wild happened upon some maidens dancing in a forest cottage. Thoroughly enchanted, he seized one and made love to her—only to discover to his everlasting horror that the lovely maiden had turned into a hideous old witch. Most witches, the demonologists agreed, also engaged in couplings with sexually active male demons, called incubi, and at times with the devil himself. Indeed, amorous seduction by the Prince of Darkness was a common method of recruiting innocent females into his sinister coterie.

Equally abhorrent was the thought that large companies of witches would regularly gather to engage in profane rites of devil worship. The English cleric Walter Map, writing in the late twelfth century, described how such an event might take place. The Satanic worshipers would meet in a secluded house with gates, doors, and windows securely fastened. After a period of silent meditation, the devil himself would appear in the shape of a monstrous black cat, sliding down a rope from the ceiling. The congregation would snuff out the candles, hum evil chants, and gather around the cat to kiss it in the most obscene places—its filthy feet, its genitals, even under its tail. Then everyone would grab his or her neighbor for a communal orgy of unbridled lust.

This blasphemous parody of Christian rites would later be termed a sabbat, apparently for the Jewish sabbath, which inspired only slightly less revulsion in the popular mind of Christian Europe. The witches' sabbat was regarded as the very apex—or nadir—of Satanism. Subsequent writers would embroider the scene with ghastly details. They would claim that the devil might reveal himself as a goat, or a toad, or an enormous black man, that male celebrants might copulate with their mothers, or with their daughters, or with other men, and that women made no distinction as to the age, sex, or familial relationship between themselves and their partners. Along with such sex-

ual license there would be frantic dancing and gluttonous feasting, as likely as not on the roasted limbs of infants they had murdered.

Eventually, the profane rituals were expanded to include a reiteration of the devil's pact. The communicants would defile the Christian sacraments, spit on the cross, denounce Christ, and swear fealty to Satan. And in a twisted parody of the Catholic confession, each individual would be called upon to relate all the evil deeds he or she had committed since the last meeting.

The irony of these descriptions is that for many centuries they had applied not to witches but to another category of Church enemy. Even worse than paganism, in the view of Church fathers, was heresy—unauthorized variances of doctrine or lapses of belief within the Church that could lead to schisms. Since Christianity's earliest days, ecclesiastical rebels of various sorts had taken issue with the central hierarchy and had broken away to form their own sects. Such splinter groups had formed new sects in Turkey and Armenia, and as the Church struggled to suppress them, it had leveled a number of fantastic charges that included devil worship, incest, infanticide, and cannibalism.

Armenian heretics known as Paulicians—and labeled sons of Satan by their enemies—were said to engage in frequent intercourse with their own mothers. The bastard offspring of these ungodly unions would then be tossed from hand to hand like footballs until they expired. After this heartless sport, the blood would be drained from their lifeless bodies and kneaded with flour to create Satanic communion wafers.

Other heresies brought forth even more imaginative charges. Some Bulgarians who split away from the Eastern Orthodox church in the tenth century were accused of child murder of the cruelest type. After an initial bloodletting, the babies, still alive and squealing, would be cast into a fire. Their ashes would be mixed with their drained blood, and the resulting potion would then be used to sauce food and drink. (An irony in this whole grim fantasy is that the first

Christians, in the days of their persecution by Roman emperors, were also accused of drinking blood, eating the flesh of children, and engaging in sexual debauches with their nearest kinsmen.)

Amid the tumult of the Middle Ages, the demons of heresy marched west through Europe, gathering adherents and disrupting the rule of the Roman church. Many of the heretics were simple, well-meaning clerics who wished only to reform what they regarded as excesses within the Church. The Vatican was a political state as well as a spiritual one, and over time, the popes had come to surround themselves with imperial splendor; moreover, Church leaders were directing their energies as much to court intrigue as to the saving of souls. The reformers demanded a return to the simple piety of Jesus and his disciples.

The Church's reaction was to hold the first mass heresy trial of medieval times, at Orléans in 1022. The defendants were reformists who preached that the Church was not necessary because the kingdom of God was in the hearts of the saved. The accusations were familiar: nocturnal flights to secret meetings, the summoning of demons and spirits, incestuous orgies. The defendants, confident of their righteousness, willingly confessed that they often met with a spirit of sorts—the Holy Ghost. They also claimed to experience visions in which they felt themselves being transported to beatific realms. Condemned to the stake, they went to their deaths singing God's praises with joyful voices and laughing, firm in their conviction that the Holy Ghost would save them.

Other heretical groups were not disposed of so easily. Among the most worrisome were the Cathars, who embraced an extreme asceticism and spread their doctrine across much of the Continent in the twelfth and thirteenth centuries. The Cathars maintained that the entire physical world was evil and Satan was its ruler. All worldly institutions, all works of art, the body and its pleasures—all these were devices created by the devil for the sole purpose of entrapping human souls. By this logic, the Catholic church was itself the devil's instrument, and all its sacraments abominations. The Cathars did not marry or procreate, since the making of babies simply imprisoned yet more souls in flesh. And so stoic were they that some chose endura, a sanctified form of suicide by starvation, in order to escape persecution.

The Catharistic heresy gained an enormous following in the south of France, where many nobles embraced the faith. Centered at Albi in Provence, its adherents became known as Albigenses, and their growing prominence became an intolerable insult to Catholic power. Unable to discourage the Cathars by other means, Pope Innocent III decided to use force. He organized a crusade, and in 1209 an army of knights and mercenaries from northern France swept into Provence, bearing the flag of the papacy and the French fleur-de-lis. The conflict raged for two full decades, reducing one of France's richest and loveliest regions to ruins. The Albigenses were conquered, but the movement persisted; it simply went underground in Provence and in other regions.

Determined to root it out once and for all, the next pope, Gregory IX, sent out an army of Dominican friars to quiz suspected heretics on their religious beliefs. Followers of Catharism and other unauthorized sects were given a month's grace, during which they might come forward and freely recant. After that, the friars started summoning suspects to a formal tribunal.

The procedures were not pleasant. The trials were conducted in secret, without benefit of a jury, and no one was allowed to confront his or her accusers or was even informed who they might be. Every available means was used to extract confessions, since under canon law the defendants could not otherwise be convicted. An army of torturers labored diligently to this end. Once the accused had admitted guilt, they were either fined or thrown into prison while authorities confiscated all of their property. Since forfeited property went to the Church, there was every reason for Church authorities to secure convictions. The ultimate penalty was burning at the stake, a foretaste of hell's fire that was administered to anyone who was foolish enough to recant a confession.

Thus, by papal decree in 1233, began the Inquisition, the official arm of Vatican law enforcement. Over the next five centuries this dread institution would consume the Church's enemies, both heretics and witches, by the hundreds of thousands. In Provence, the Inquisition erased the Cathars from the face of the earth. The Church soon extended it to other parts of France, then to Italy and Germany. In the latter realm, Emperor Frederick II had already launched a similar campaign, assigning his secular officers to the task of rooting out heretics; now his prosecutors began collaborating with those of the Church. In Spain, the royal family established its own independent Inquisition, using the same brutal methods to prosecute Moors, Jews, heretics, and occasional groups of suspected witches. And so was launched a tradition of wholesale slaughter, of tortured bodies and burning flesh, a legacy that denied the basic precepts of civilized society.

One particularly zealous prosecutor was Conrad of Marburg, who was appointed chief inquisitor of Germany under an agreement between Frederick II and Pope Gregory. A thin-lipped man of austere tastes, Conrad focused on various heretical groups in Alsace and the Rhineland, relying on a network of assistants and paid informers that were as fanatical as himself. Not content with the more obvious forms of apostasy, he leveled accusations against anyone he could, wringing out evidence by bribing witnesses and torturing suspects. A reign of terror ensued, in which brothers were forced to denounce brothers, wives their husbands, peasants their lords. "We would gladly burn a hundred," explained a deputy, "if just one among them was guilty."

Eventually Conrad went too far. He chose as his target a devout and influential nobleman, Count Henry of Sayn, who according to witnesses had been seen riding to a diabolic orgy on the back of a giant crab. The count had powerful friends in the Church hierarchy—he had endowed several monasteries—and they made certain that his name was cleared. Shortly afterward, Conrad was found murdered on the road between Marburg and Mainz.

The Inquisition was to be a crucial factor in changing Europe's treatment of alleged witches, not least because of the judicial procedure it employed. Before the Inquisition got underway, charges of maleficium—as with all criminal charges—could be brought only through an accusatory procedure. This meant that a private individual, not an official acting on behalf of the state, the Church, or society, had to come forth and accuse the supposed evildoer.

The judicial practices of the day dictated that from then on, the accuser was virtually as much on trial as was the accused. If the defendant had to be locked up to ensure his or her presence in court, then the accuser was jailed too, to keep matters even. And the accuser had to make the case against the accused; there was no official prosecutor to help. Finally, if the judge was not convinced and found the defendant innocent, then the person who had brought the accusation could be subjected to as great a punishment as would have been dealt to the accused if found guilty. Needless to say, few souls were brave enough to accuse another of a crime—especially not the crime of maleficium, which, being of an occult, nonmaterial nature, was extremely difficult to prove.

The new inquisitorial procedure changed all that. No individual had to take personal responsibility for an accusation. Instead, men of the Church, secure in their positions and for the most part beyond reach of retaliation, served as judges and prosecutors, calling in and questioning defendants and witnesses, ordering the extraction of confessions and other testimony by torture if necessary, reaching verdicts, and passing sentences. Obviously the Inquisition could be a powerful device to use against witches should the Church wish to turn it to that end.

At first there was no formal pronouncement linking heresy with witchcraft, but the parallels were only too apparent. It took no great leap of imagination to spot the connection between a devil-worshiping, child-murdering heretic and a night-flying, Satan-loving, sex-crazed sorcerer

In Goya's late-eighteenth-century painting A Scene from the Inquisition, *four defendants wearing the conical*

hats that designated heretics and witches face the smug, self-righteous clerics of the Spanish Inquisition.

with a taste for human flesh. Suggestive passages began occurring in Church documents: A notice circulated in 1240 among members of the Cistercian order referred to sorcery as "a kind of heretical depravity." In 1258, a group of inquisitors requested that they be allowed to extend their purview and go after witches. Then in 1320, the last links were forged. Attempts had been made on the life of Pope John XXII, involving poison and, it was alleged, witchcraft. The pope ordered all of his inquisitors to see to it that "witches, the infectors of God's flock, flee from the House of God." From that point on, the statutes against heretics would be applied with equal force to the alleged crime of witchcraft.

By an odd turn of circumstances, the first witch trial in an ecclesiastical court took place in Ireland, home of elves and fairy queens at the far edge of Christendom, where the Inquisition had never really penetrated. In the town of Kil-

In the 1579 woodcut below, a youth spies on a group of witches who are preparing for sabbat. One hag stirs a flying ointment as another applies it to her leg. Those who already have partaken of the magic salve soar up the chimney and off into the sky.

kenny there lived a wealthy and well-bred matron, Dame Alice Kyteler, now married to her fourth husband. Each of her former spouses had bequeathed her his fortune when he died, and her present husband presumably would do the same. Dame Alice, in turn, was expected to bestow her property on her son by her first marriage, William Outlawe—thereby depriving her several stepchildren of any inheritance at all.

Her present husband was now wasting away from a curious disease that had caused his hair and fingernails to fall out. The husband apparently thought his illness a natural one, until, at the suggestion of a maidservant, he forced open a number of personal storage chests belonging to Dame Alice. Inside one of them, he found a collection of mysterious powders and ointments indicative of sorcery and, according to one account, a wafer of sac-

ramental bread with the devil's name stamped on it. It suddenly seemed obvious that Dame Alice had bewitched him, and her previous husbands as well, so that she could inherit the men's money.

This bizarre intelligence and the chest's items were delivered to the local bishop, Richard de Ledrede, an English Franciscan who had trained in France and had come away burning with inquisitorial fervor. De Ledrede already suspected that

The dissection of a dead witch reveals a large toad in place of her heart—evidence of an inhuman nature—in this Swiss woodcut from about 1500. Regarded as revolting, evil creatures, toads were one of the forms thought to be favored by shapeshifting demons.

witches were abroad in his diocese. Here now was the evidence he sought. He indicted Dame Alice and ten alleged accomplices on seven counts of witchcraft and heresy, bolstering his case with testimony obtained through torture of a lady's maid from Dame Alice's house, Petronilla de Meath.

Besides using sorcery to murder her husband, said the bishop, Dame Alice had denied God, defiled the sacraments, sought knowledge of the future, and performed demonic parodies of Christian rites that ended with the cry, "Fie! Fie! Fie! Amen!" The woman was also accused of sacrificing roosters to a petty demon named Robin, who was the son of another demon, Art.

Moreover, she was said to have taken the said Artisson (as Robin's patronymic was styled) in various forms into her bed—at times he was a cat, or a shaggy black dog, or a black dwarf who carried an iron rod. To work their spells, Dame Alice and her group had supposedly concocted ointments from the intestines of the sacrificial roosters, which they mixed with herbs, spiders, black worms, the flesh of serpents, the hair and nails of corpses, and the brains of unbaptized children, all boiled together over an oak fire in

the skull of a thief who had been beheaded.

The bishop first attempted to press these charges with the civil authorities—who, as it happened, were all either friends or relatives of Dame Alice. Much to his chagrin, the prelate's case was thrown out of court. Incensed, he excommunicated Dame Alice, cited her son William for heresy, and placed the entire diocese under interdict, which excluded the faithful from access to the sacraments.

Finally a compromise was reached. Dame Alice received a court summons but was allowed to escape to England. William submitted to a few weeks in jail. And the bishop was permitted to vent his wrath on Dame Alice's purported accomplices. One in particular bore the brunt, the maid Petronilla. She was flogged six times and confessed to whatever the bishop wished: She admitted making sacrifices to Artisson and attending nocturnal orgies. In addition, she described Dame Alice as a most wicked and despicable witch. The unfortunate Petronilla was excommunicated and burned alive on November 3, 1324, the first victim of the witch hunt in Ireland.

As it turned out, the Kyteler affair was an isolated event in Ireland; the witch craze never achieved its full fury in that land. But on the Continent, Pope John's decree set off a spate of witch trials—including some involving clerics who took too keen an interest in sorcery. At Agen in southwestern France, a canon, another priest, and a layman were accused in 1326 of calling forth demons to kill people and make storms. The canon was allegedly caught in possession of books about magic as well as containers of peculiar powders and stinking liquids. His co-conspirators were said to have stolen limbs and heads from corpses on the local gallows for use in magic rituals. The layman was burned to death, while the clerics were turned over to Church authorities. Their fate is not known. Also undocumented is the fate of a prior and two other priests who were similarly charged that same year with practicing magic and summoning demons and who were handed over to a commission of three cardinals.

In 1323, the inquisitor of Paris hauled into court an abbot, several canons, and two laymen—the laymen being a magician and his assistant. The abbot had lost some valuables, and as would many of his contemporaries in an era when magical powers were often taken for granted, he turned to a sorcerer to help find them. Unfortunately for the abbot, he was not paying sufficient heed to the Church's new attitude about such matters. He and the other clerics were stripped of their priesthoods and imprisoned for the rest of their lives. The magician and his accomplice were burned to death.

A few years later a Carmelite brother in the southern French town of Carcassonne was brought before the Inquisition for allegedly using sorcery to satisfy his sexual appetite. The monk, named Pierre Recordi, confessed mixing blood from toads and his own saliva into wax puppets, then placing them under the thresholds of women's houses. Subsequently, if a woman did not comply with his advances, she would be persecuted by a demon. Recordi's confession was probably elicited by torture; during his long trial he several times recanted it. But nonetheless he was sentenced to life imprisonment, during which he was to be chained hand and foot and given nothing but bread and water.

In Switzerland, scores of accused witches were tried in secular courts. At Simmental, near Bern, an unspecified number of victims went to the stake convicted of boldly offering homage to Satan during Sunday church services. These witches also stole children, the charges read, and cooked and ate them for lunch, after first draining their blood to make magic ointments. Rubbed onto the body, the ointment could render the parishioners invisible, or transform them into animals, or allow them to fly through the air in proper witch style.

The secular courts of northern France also turned their attention to crimes of heretical witchcraft. In a Paris trial that began in 1390, a thirty-four-year-old female fortuneteller named Jehanne de Brigue, known for some reason as la Cordière, "the ropemaker," was accused of bewitching one Jehan de Ruilly at the behest of de Ruilly's disaffected wife, Macette. The wife, it was charged, had fallen in love with a handsome young curate and in order to pursue her romance with him had employed the witch to turn off de Ruilly's affections. La Cordière obliged, but her incantations made the poor man so ill that the remorseful witch restored de Ruilly to health.

In the Paris criminal court, la Cordière first denied everything. Then, under severe questioning, she admitted casting spells by invoking the Holy Trinity, neglecting her regular prayers, and not washing on Sunday. Pressed further, she confessed that her aunt had taught her how to call up a demon named Haussibut and that she sometimes worked magic by suckling toads and sticking pins in wax dolls. The trial dragged on through winter and spring, with occasional recesses. At one point in the proceedings, la Cordière was sentenced to burning but was granted a reprieve because she was thought to be pregnant.

Eventually, the fortuneteller implicated Macette, who was arrested and charged. Tortured on the rack, Macette confessed to having played a part in the affair, and she, too, was found guilty. There were further delays. La Cordière's sentence had been reinstated, but she appealed to the Parliament of Paris, the nation's highest tribunal. Another set of judges reviewed the case. Finally, it confirmed both verdicts. On August 19, 1391, the two women were taken to the Pig Market. There they were burned at the stake, possibly after having first been garroted, although the record is not clear on this point.

The Paris civil trial had lasted nearly a year, and it taxed the brains and consciences of the country's top ju-

---

A mob of misshapen, grotesquely ugly witches huddle before the devil, who has taken the form of a large he-goat—a frequent guise—in Francisco de Goya's 1822 mural called The Witches' Sabbath. In this rendering of witches' pagan worship, an attractive young maiden holding a muff, perhaps a novice witch, sits apart from the crowd (right). Like the hags, she seems mesmerized by the chilling scene, in which a figure shrouded in white rises from what looks like a grave.

rists. By contrast, the Church's Inquisition dispensed its own unique justice with the speed of God's own thunderbolt. There were no appeals, no second thoughts. A sect called the Waldenses—named for their founder, Peter Waldo, who had translated the New Testament without authorization—had been a target for Church persecution since before the Inquisition actually began. The Inquisition pursued the Waldensians, whose itinerant preachers adhered to vows of poverty, into almost every corner of Europe. Typical was the fate of Waldensians who had sought refuge in the rugged Dauphiné region of the French Alps. In 1428, the Inquisition closed in on them with charges of invoking demons, stirring up storms, eating human flesh, and indulging in other witchlike and heretical behavior. Before the hunt finished, 110 Waldensian women and 57 men had been convicted and roasted alive.

Even among the upper reaches of Church hierarchy—at times, perhaps, especially there—no one was safe from the lightning of the Inquisition. Father Guillaume Adeline was prior of an important monastery at St.-Germain-en-Laye. He was also a noted doctor of theology who formerly had taught in Paris. Maybe some rival theologian had it in for Adeline. In any case, in 1453, he was accused of witchcraft. Inquisitors alleged that a written compact with the devil was found on his person. Eventually, almost certainly after extensive torture, he confessed. To such an intellectual—even one caught up in pain and peril—the offenses he was compelled to admit must have seemed ironically ludicrous: making love to a succubus, flying on a broomstick, and kissing a goat under its tail.

A single random accusation, if properly nurtured by the Inquisition's prosecutors and torturers, could lead to the

A 1566 English chapbook, or pamphlet, details the trial and confession of accused witch Agnes Waterhouse. The forerunners of today's lurid tabloids, such publications helped to spread the witch hysteria throughout the Continent.

netting of scores of victims. In 1459 in the northern French city of Arras, then a great manufacturing center, a poor hermit was condemned to be burned as a witch. Seeking to save himself and avoid further torture, he eagerly denounced a prostitute and an elderly poet hitherto best known for his celebrations of the Virgin Mary. Those two in turn accused others, and soon the burnings began.

The first of the executions took place in May 1460. Four pitiful creatures, including a half-witted woman and the old poet, were led onto a platform in front of the Episcopal Palace in Arras. Dressed in robes and miters emblazoned with the devil's symbols, they listened to the charges of which they were convicted—that they had flown to sabbats on sticks, trampled the cross, and adored the devil. (To protect the tender sensibilities of those who came to witness the witches being burned alive, authorities omitted from the reading the crime of having intercourse with Satan.) Then, as the fires were lighted, the victims proclaimed their innocence, screaming with their dying breaths that they had been promised they would be allowed to live if they confessed to the charges.

The arrests in and around Arras multiplied. Anyone who spoke out against the witch hunt was soon among the prisoners. Inquisitors declared that only witches would oppose the burnings and that therefore any objectors should be burned also. According to the inquisitors, no less than a third of all people who claimed to be Chris-

While witches and demons cavort in the sky, a group of Waldensians—in reality a reform-minded Christian sect—adore the hindquarters of their devil-lord in this illustration from a fifteenth-century propaganda tract. So successful was the Church's campaign to label the heretics as devil worshipers that in certain parts of France the words for Waldensian and witch became synonymous.

59

A Gallery of English Witches

By the mid-1500s, the witch mania gripping the Continent had reached England. The women convicted of witchcraft there were mostly eccentric crones such as the ones shown in woodcuts here, linked more with simple sorcery than heresy, and usually accused of having familiars and hexing enemies. As a result, fewer English witches were tried, tortures were less barbarous, and the condemned were hanged instead of burned.

Scattering breadcrumbs inside a magic circle where demons dance with a cat and dog, Anne Bodenham of Wiltshire divines the future, an act that led to her witchcraft conviction. Although she denied any traffic with the devil, Mrs. Bodenham did indulge in the occult: She wore about her neck a toad in a green sack and advised her neighbors on medicinal herbs and poisons.

Three condemned witches dangle from the gallows in this contemporary illustration of the 1589 Chelmsford trial. One of the victims, Joan Prentice, also appears in the foreground, surrounded by the toads and various familiars—some bearing nametags—through which she and the others supposedly wrought their nefarious deeds.

A 1619 trial pamphlet depicts the three condemned hags whose testimony sealed the fates of suspected witches Joan Flower and her two daughters. Flower and daughter Margaret had been employed by the earl of Rutland, but he had dismissed Margaret from service. According to the hags, Mother Flower took steps to avenge the insult. Aided by her daughters—who both confessed—she engaged in dark rituals to destroy the earl's elder son, who indeed sickened and died. When Rutland's other son weakened, the three Flowers were arrested and convicted.

"As far from grace as heaven from hell" was how a 1612 chapbook described alleged witch Agnes Brown of Guilsborough, depicted here riding a sow with two cronies. Yet it was the unseemly behavior of her daughter, Joan Vaughan, that proved the pair's undoing. Vaughan so offended a Miss Belcher that the gentlewoman struck the girl; Vaughan vowed revenge. When Belcher took sick, she accused the ill-bred women of witchcraft. They were duly convicted and hanged.

Elizabeth Sawyer of Edmonton, hanged in 1621, was one of the few English witches to confess to traffic with the devil. She claimed he first appeared to her when she was swearing and blaspheming. Thereafter, the archfiend came to her in the form of a dog, which she suckled from a preternatural teat under her clothes. Sawyer declared that in return, the animal allegedly harmed people and beasts at her bidding.

tians, including many bishops and cardinals, were actually witches. Soon the entire city and surrounding region were in the grip of terror. Hundreds of people from all walks of life were implicated. Some of the richer folk managed to pay bribes in exchange for their freedom. Even so, several large estates were confiscated. The poor had no recourse; they filled the prisons and fueled the fires. Trade suffered, and prosperity vanished.

Eventually the authorities in Paris intervened. The chief inquisitor was summoned home, and anyone left in jail was set free. Finally, in 1491, the Paris Parliament declared that the Inquisition had acted "in error." Interrogation by torture was condemned. Those who had died at Arras were exonerated. A mass was said in their honor, and a cross was erected as a memorial on the spot where they were burned.

A reaction had in fact set in. As early as 1460, three leading French prelates had announced that witches' sabbats—a major item in the Arras charges— simply did not occur. Then in 1475, a book began to circulate that cast doubt on other aspects of witchcraft. Some years earlier the Dominican prior at Nuremberg, Johannes Nider, had written a manuscript on the witch phenomenon. Nider did not deny that there were witches or that they did the devil's work. But the idea that they flew through the air, or could transform themselves into animals, seemed to him as preposterous as it had to the author of the *Canon Episcopi* some centuries earlier. A new invention, the printing press, was coming into use; Nider's manuscript was widely distributed, and it even provoked second thoughts among numerous readers. But as with the *Canon Episcopi,* such temperate views did not survive for long.

In Germany, a pair of ardent inquisitors, Heinrich Kramer and Jakob Sprenger, were incensed that large numbers of people, including clergymen, still felt that witchcraft was neither seriously evil nor particularly widespread. Kramer and Sprenger complained directly to Pope Innocent

Judgment by a Watery Ordeal

While rumor and false witness were often the only evidence needed to convict an accused witch, various tests were devised to confirm the suspect's guilt or innocence. Among the most common of these methods was trial by water, an ancient practice mentioned as early as the second millennium BC in the Code of Hammurabi. Initially employed for all crimes, the water ordeal, or swimming, became a critical test for witches during the seventeenth century, particularly in England. If the accused floated when cast into water, she was deemed a witch and executed; if she sank, she was declared innocent. And if the suspect drowned in the process—a not unlikely outcome— at least her corpse enjoyed a proper burial. King James I gave the test royal approval, rationalizing that water would reject those who had "shaken off them the sacred water of baptism."

England officially prohibited the practice by the early 1700s, but it nonetheless lingered in folk belief as a legitimate test. Indeed, as late as 1865, two persons at Castle Hedingham near Chelmsford were brought to trial for swimming an alleged witch.

An accused witch, bundled into a gunnysack, is about to be cast into the water in this sixteenth-century woodcut. The water test was frequently employed when a suspect refused to confess, even when he or she was threatened with torture.

A 1613 English pamphlet depicts the swimming of alleged witch Mary Sutton (right). The men holding on to her ropes will retrieve her if she sinks.

In this nineteenth-century rendition of a swimming test, a suspected witch floats guiltily while another recedes into the deep. Witches were generally bound hand to foot before dunking, a practice that not only restrained them but also kept a surprising number of them afloat.

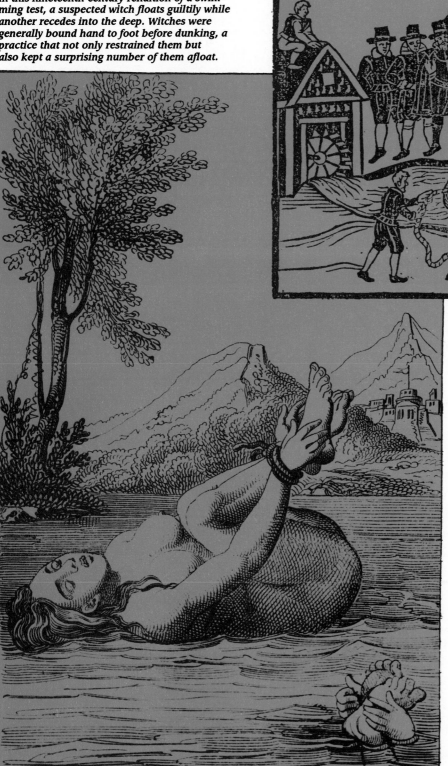

Other Damning Determinations

Witch hunters had means other than the water trial of certifying their prey. For instance, a terrified suspect's inability to weep on demand incriminated her, since witches were thought unable to shed tears. Quite common also was the search for witch's marks—extra nipples at which she supposedly suckled her familiars—and devil's marks, insensitive spots on the skin allegedly made by the devil's claws or teeth. Suspects were stripped, shaved from head to toe, then exhaustively examined for blemishes, moles, or scars that could be labeled diabolical. To find marks invisible to the eye, examiners prodded every inch of the accused's body with a bodkin until they found a spot that did not bleed or feel pain. Scholars now say the emotional shock of being publicly stripped and searched could well have produced areas of temporary anesthesia in some victims, thus providing witch hunters with the "proof" they sought.

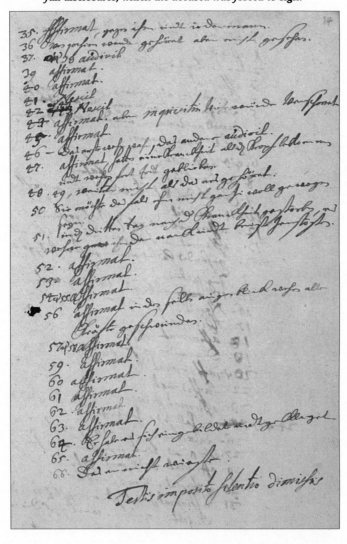

VIII, who reacted with anger and alarm to their reports of a lack of concern about witches. Thus encouraged, Kramer and Sprenger produced an exhaustive tome—*Malleus Maleficarum,* or "Hammer of Witches"—and affixed to it a papal bull Innocent had written, exploiting that document as if it were some kind of endorsement for their book.

Malleus Maleficarum was printed in 1486. If the floodgates of witch-hunt hysteria had been closing, the book reopened them wide. Innocent's papal bull, the first Vatican decree to be widely circulated in print, called upon all Christians to support his inquisitors. Should anyone be less than cooperative, it warned, "upon him shall fall the wrath of God Almighty." Any doubt that witches existed, or that they consorted with the devil, was itself heresy.

biblical injunction, in Exodus 22:18, that "thou shalt not suffer a witch to live."

The authors added another stroke to the darkening portrait of the classic witch. Besides their abhorrence of demonic sin, they had an abiding disdain for the entire female gender. "What else is a woman but a foe to friendship," the writers asked, "an inescapable punishment, a necessary evil, a natural temptation?" Women were lustful, false, vain, vindictive, mean-minded, and weak-willed. Ever since Eve offered Adam the apple, they had lured men to perdition. No wonder the devil sought them out. Thousands of men would expire in the witch hunt. But the great majority of victims would henceforth be women.

The *Malleus* was printed and reprinted again and again over the next two centuries, there was a total of thirteen editions by 1520 and sixteen more by 1669. Originally written in Latin, the book was translated for popular consumption into German, French, Italian, and English. And the work engraved on the European consciousness the indelible image of the devil-worshiping, night-flying, curse-spouting female witch.

In their impassioned screed of 250,000 words, Kramer and Sprenger detailed everything known or imagined about witches and witchcraft. The work ranged from biblical times to the present moment, blending folk beliefs about sorcery with Church doctrine on heresy and demon worship. After theory came practice, with legal guidelines for conducting trials, examining witnesses, and obtaining confessions. In addition, there were some helpful suggestions on the most effective types of torture. The *Malleus* became a handbook for persecution, with a single goal in mind: To enforce the

Even as the Catholic church accelerated its campaign to rid the world of witches, its weightiest earthbound enemy joined in the struggle. In the sixteenth century the Protes-

In the atmosphere of suspicion pervading Germany during the witch hysteria, the slightest deviation from the norm merited punishment, as evidenced by the shame masks shown here. The masks were designed to mirror the offense: Masks featuring long ears, such as the ones at left and bottom left, indicated eavesdropping; the long-nosed mask below signaled nosiness; and venomous talkers might have to wear a snake-tongued mask such as the one at bottom center. Offenders were locked into the iron headgear—which often had sharp inner spikes and blades that were forced into the wearer's mouth—then staked out in the town square for public ridicule.

tant Reformation succeeded in accomplishing what all previous schisms had failed to do: It split western Europe's branch of Christianity into two opposing camps. But Martin Luther, whose attacks on Church corruption brought this about, had no quarrel with the Roman church's attitude toward witchcraft; he considered witches to be as dangerous as Catholics did. And he knew firsthand of the devil's wiles, having wrestled long and hard against them in the depths of his own soul. "I should have no compassion on these witches," Luther once declared; "I would burn all of them." Nor did his fellow Protestant John Calvin show any greater tolerance for witches; like Luther, he regarded them only as perilous. When Calvin heard that there were witches practicing in Geneva, which he governed as an independent theocracy, he sought out the alleged malefactors and condemned them to the fires.

Elsewhere in Europe the witch craze continued to flare up first in one place, then in another, often in the wake of drought, flood, or some other natural disaster, or as an outgrowth of a political or religious conflict, such as the sporadic clashes of Catholics versus Protestants. In Alsace and Lorraine and in the Rhineland states of western Germany, the trials multiplied until entire populations lived in mortal fear. In 1556, a woman at Bievres in northern France was mistakenly burned alive, instead of being garroted first as her sentence required. When it was discovered that she had suffered the more agonizing punishment, which was usually reserved for convicted witches who recanted their confessions, inquisitors airily dismissed the error as God's secret judgment. In 1579, the Church Council at Melun declared: "Every charlatan and diviner, and others who practice necromancy, pyromancy, chiromancy, hydromancy, will be punished by death."

Among the witch hunt's most energetic practitioners was a grim zealot named Nicholas Remy, who in 1591 became Lorraine's attorney general. As a youth, Remy had been intrigued by the witchcraft trials and executions in the villages of his native Vosges Mountains. He later became personally involved when, as a lawyer, he prosecuted a

The Price of Pain

A grim indication of the businesslike nature of witch trials in Europe was the custom of charging the accused or her family a fee for every act of barbarous abuse she endured, from imprisonment to execution. Even after the witchcraft craze abated, the practice continued for other alleged criminals. As late as 1757, the archbishop of Cologne saw fit to itemize the costs of torture to prevent executioners from overcharging. Excerpts from the chilling list appear below. Fees are expressed in reichsthalers, German empire coins, each containing an ounce of pure silver, and albus, local units of currency, each worth one seventy-eighth of a reichsthaler.

	Reichsthaler	Albus
For beheading and burning, everything included	5	26
For the necessary rope for this procedure, and for preparing and igniting the stake	2	0
For strangling and burning	4	0
For rope and for preparing and igniting the stake	2	0
For burning alive	4	0
For rope and for preparing and igniting the stake	2	0
For breaking alive on the wheel	4	0
For rope and chains for this procedure	2	0
For setting up the body which is tied to the wheel	2	52
For cutting off a hand or several fingers and for beheading, all together	3	26
The same: in addition, for burning with a hot iron	1	26
For the necessary rope and cloth	1	26
Before the actual execution starts, for squeezing the delinquent with red-hot tongs, apart from the above-mentioned fee for hanging, for every application	0	26
For cutting out the tongue entirely, or part of it, and after-		

	Reichsthaler	Albus
ward for burning the mouth with a red-hot iron	5	0
For this procedure, the usual rope, tongs, and knife	2	0
For nailing to the gallows a cut-off tongue or a chopped-off hand	1	26
For flogging in jail, including the rods	1	0
For thrashing	0	52
For putting in the pillory	0	52
For putting in the pillory, and for whipping, including the rope and the rods	1	26
For terrorizing by showing the instruments of torture	1	0
For the first degree of torture	1	26
For arranging and crushing the thumb for this degree	0	26
For the second degree of torture, including setting the limbs afterward, and for salve which is used	2	26
Should, however, a person be tortured in both degrees of torture, the executioner is to get for both degrees performed at the same time, setting the limbs afterward and for use of the salve, for all this he should be paid	6	0

In this etching of a 1549 Amsterdam witch burning, six innocents perish at the stakes—a fate for which the victims paid a hefty fee.

*In this seventeenth-century engraving of a classical scene, execu-
tioners thrust a victim into the ovenlike belly of a fire-scorched bronze bull. The
device, which dates from about 550 BC, was rediscovered by
torturers during the witch-trial era.*

beggar woman for bewitching his own son. It appears that Remy had refused to give the woman alms, and he then considered her responsible some days afterward when the boy took ill and died.

From then on he was a relentless demonologist—the term applied to lawyers, judges, or theologians who specialized in witches and sorcery. He tracked down every strange coincidence or event on the theory that since God must be rational, "whatever is not normal is due to the devil." In a book he wrote on the subject, he declared that "everything which is unknown lies, as far as I am concerned, in the cursed domain of demonology; for there are no unexplained facts." When he published his book in 1595, he boasted on the title page that he had condemned some 900 witches in fifteen years. Remy continued to exterminate witches for al-

most two decades more, until he passed away in 1612.

Another who showed no qualms about the numbers he sent to their deaths was Henri Bouget, chief judge of Saint Claude in the French province of Burgundy. He employed the Inquisition's cruelest methods to wrest confessions from 600 people, ranging from elderly invalids to prepubescent children. It troubled him not at all to include children, believing that once they fell into the grip of Satan, they seldom could be reformed. All too many of Bouget's victims, young and old, were burned alive. One poor woman found the strength to burst her bonds at the stake three times and three times was tied up again and thrust back into the flames.

Despite the excesses of Remy and Bouget, they did not pursue their callings with more vigor and relish than did

Pierre de Lancre, who was appointed special prosecutor in the Basque region of southwestern France in 1609. De Lancre probably stands alone for the very scale of his heinous vision. His investigations convinced him that *everybody*, the entire population of 30,000 souls in his district—including all the clergy—had been converted to witchcraft. The devils who had worked this wondrously wicked deed, he said, had arrived in the guise of refugees from Japan and the East Indies. Witnesses, he averred, had sighted flocks of Basque witches flying off to sabbats as far away as Newfoundland. A more frequent venue was the main square at Bordeaux, where de Lancre claimed sabbat attendance reached as high as 100,000.

De Lancre worked swiftly, and in scarcely four months, he later boasted, he cremated 600 people. The numbers were great enough to inspire one of those rare instances when a community rose up in revolt against the witch hunt. Mobs of howling protesters rioted and converged on his courthouse. Clearly, the devil had urged them on—or so the prosecutor believed. And after de Lancre burned three priests, the bishop of Bayonne himself rescued five others from the prosecutor's jail and joined the opposition to the witch hunt.

De Lancre's work apparently continued, however, because in 1612, he published a book describing it. For other would-be witch hunters, the book provided rich details of the standard allegations that were the stuff of the trials. The devil first appears as a black man and at midnight makes a pact with the accused. The witch finds himself or herself able to fly all over the world to Friday night sabbats, where the devil—now in the shape of a huge black goat—copulates with the women. Then the participants fling themselves into indiscriminate sex, eat human infants, cook up poisonous plants and bits of corpses that they dug up from graveyards, and set forth to kill people and livestock and to destroy crops.

Despite de Lancre's grandiose ambitions, even in his district the persecution mania failed to reach the savage proportions it achieved in the German states. A series of calamities struck the region around the city of Trier in 1580—heavy rains, plagues of mice and grasshoppers, forays by Protestant mercenaries—and the troubles continued throughout the decade. Authorities blamed witchcraft and commenced trials in both civil and ecclesiastical courts. Convictions eliminated two villages, virtually wiping them from the map, and in another, only two members of the entire female population remained alive. The victims included some of the state's highest officials—burgomasters, counselors, judges.

Among the last was Trier's chief civil magistrate, Dietrich Flade, whose own moderation in handling trials had angered some authorities. His record of convictions was suspiciously meager. Could the judge be a witch himself? The Church inquisitors produced a befuddled boy who swore that he had seen Flade at a sabbat; and an old crone who was about to be executed gladly testified that Flade was a witch, in order to secure for herself the mercy of strangulation before roasting. Under torture, the judge confessed to plotting against the archbishop of Trier and to throwing clods of dirt into the air, which turned into crop-destroying slugs. Found guilty, he was strangled to death and his body burned.

The pyres at Trier were the initial sparks of a conflagration that swept through many German states. In the Saxon town of Quedlinburg, the executioner burned 133 witches on a single day in 1589. A year later, a writer commented that in the town of Wolfenbüttel "the place of execution looked like a small wood from the number of stakes." At Fulda to the south, a sadistic judge named Balthasar Ross executed 300 people between 1603 and 1606, after first hoisting the women up on the pulley-and-rope device called the strappado, their wrists tied behind their backs, and jabbing hot skewers through their flesh. Ross met his own fate a few years later, when he was sent to the scaffold for embezzling state funds.

Among the most brutally efficient German witch hunters were two cousins, each ruler of his own state. During the 1620s, Philipp Adolf von Ehrenberg, prince-bishop of Würzburg, burned 900 local witches; his cousin Johann Georg II, Fuchs von Dornheim, of Bamberg, did away with 600 *(page 91)*. Würzburg's horrified chancellor documented what it was like: "A third of the city is surely implicated. The richest, most attractive, most prominent of the clergy are already executed. A week ago, a girl of nineteen was burned, said everywhere to be the fairest in the whole city ... there are 300 children of three or four years who are said to have intercourse with the devil. I have seen children of seven put to death, and brave little scholars of ten, twelve, fourteen." Among the victims was the prince-bishop's sole heir, Ernest, a university student whose worst crimes seemed to have been a taste for Würzburg beer and an eye for older women.

Confessions were still mandatory before an execution could take place, and the German inquisitors developed the process of extracting them to a high art. While imprisoned, the victims were force-fed herring cooked in salt to induce a raging thirst, for which they were of course denied water. At the appointed hour, the victims were stripped—and in many cases, the women raped—before being led into the torture chamber, where notaries waited to take down their every agonized word. All the torture instruments had been blessed by a priest beforehand.

The torturers might begin with thumbscrews, followed by several dozen lashes from a whip. Then came leg vises, in which tightened metal bands crushed the shins and ankles, after which there might be a period of stretching on the rack or hanging from ropes to dislocate the shoulders. If these methods proved inadequate in securing a confession, the accused would be submerged in ice water, or a scalding bath laced with lime, or have sulfur-dipped feathers burned under their

Weighing the Evidence

To fly through the air, the wisdom of the era held, witches had to be preternaturally light. Following that logic, weighing the accused became a popular method of witch detection in Europe. The tests varied from town to town. In one village, the suspect might be weighed against the big bible in the parish church; if the scales tipped in her favor, she was deemed innocent. Elsewhere she might be required to balance the scales exactly against a set weight—a near-impossible feat ensuring a guilty verdict. There was one place, however, where a judgment of innocence was virtually guaranteed—the Dutch town of Oudewater. Under the watchful, honest eyes of the weighmasters, as depicted in the 1887 illustration below, suspects were measured against their minimum nonflying weight. Since that number was determined by a simple formula based on height, everyone outweighed the minimum, and not one person was convicted of witchcraft in Oudewater.

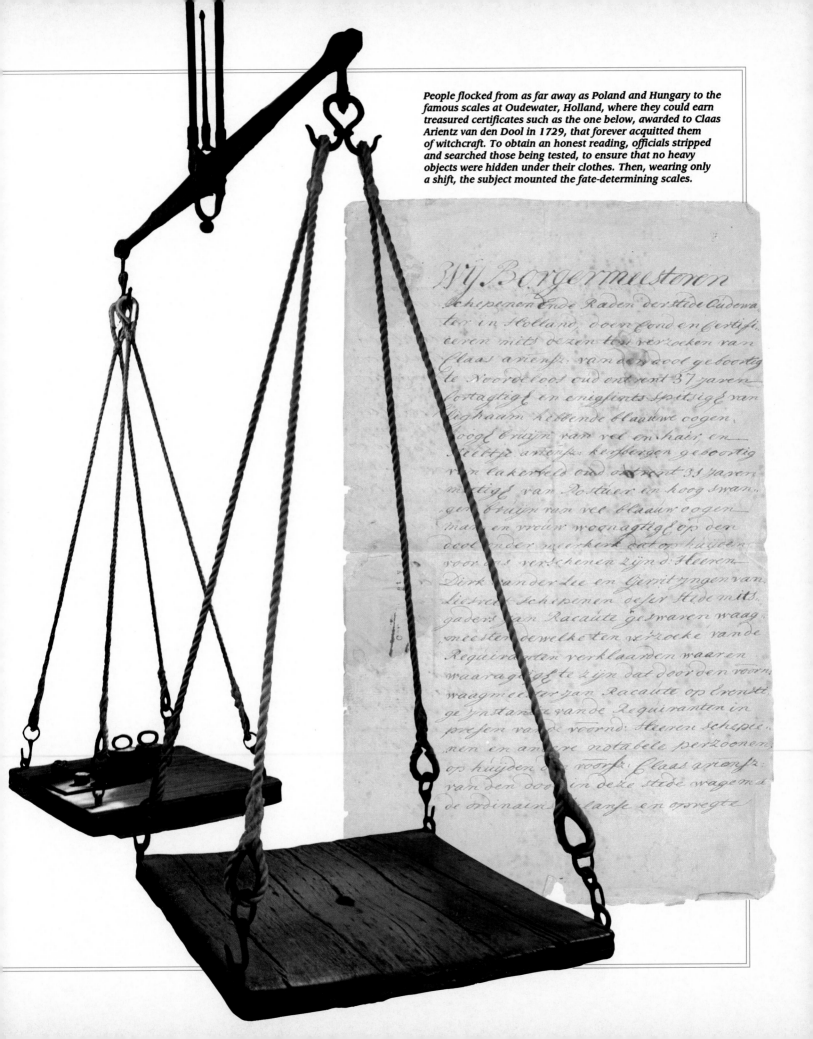

People flocked from as far away as Poland and Hungary to the famous scales at Oudewater, Holland, where they could earn treasured certificates such as the one below, awarded to Claas Arientz van den Dool in 1729, that forever acquitted them of witchcraft. To obtain an honest reading, officials stripped and searched those being tested, to ensure that no heavy objects were hidden under their clothes. Then, wearing only a shift, the subject mounted the fate-determining scales.

groin and armpits. One or another horrifying device persuaded most suspects to say whatever was necessary to put an end to the suffering.

Once a confession was extracted, there was no going back. In one account, a woman named Margaret confessed to various crimes after being subjected to fiendish torture. The torturer then threatened her, saying, "You have now made your confession. Will you deny it? Tell me now, and if so, I will give you another going over. If you recant tomorrow or the day after tomorrow, or before the court, you will come back again into my hands, and then you will learn that up to now I have only been playing with you. I will plague you and torture you in such a way that even a stone would cry out in pity."

A few hardy souls resisted to the end. The judicial reports told of a remarkable sixty-nine-year-old German widow, Clara Geissler, who withstood the thumbscrews, but when "her feet were crushed and her body stretched" on the rack, confessed to everything she was accused of: that she drank the blood of infants she had stolen on night flights and that she had murdered sixty babies. Under prodding, she named twenty other women who had acted as accomplices and declared that the widow of a prominent burgomaster had presided over the night flights. Yet upon her release from the rack, Clara immediately retracted her confessions. She was then tortured a second time and confessed again, only to recant once more. The third time, she was tortured with "utmost severity," said the report. Her agony continued for several hours, at the end of which she collapsed and died. "The Devil would not let her reveal anything more and so wrung her neck," concluded the report, in tones of disappointment.

And while the victims screamed and perished, their prosecutors and executioners grew rich. Not only did convicted witches and other heretics forfeit their estates, they had to pay all trial expenses, as well as fees for every torture inflicted upon them *(page 66)*. At Trier, a chronicler noted, "the executioner rode a blooded horse, like a noble of the court, and went clad in gold and silver; his wife vied with noble dames in the richness of her array." If the witch had no money, as was often the case, the populace paid for the trial and torture through assessments.

The horror of the witch trials and the calamitous effect they had on economies throughout Europe inevitably led to a reaction among those with the courage to speak out. One of the relatively few voices raised in protest in early-seventeenth-century Germany was the leading Jesuit official at Würzburg, Friedrich von Spee. Among Spee's priestly duties was hearing the last confessions of condemned prisoners, and he soon came to the realization that virtually all those accused of demonic practices were in fact completely innocent. "Previously I never thought of doubting that there were many witches in the world," he wrote. "Now, however, when I examine the public record, I find myself believing that there are hardly any." In 1631, he published a book, *Cautio Criminalis,* or "Precautions for Prosecutors," that condemned torture and called for rational trial procedures with fair use of evidence and defense attorneys for the accused. "Grief has turned my hair white," he lamented, "grief for the witches I have accompanied to the stake." (But there were limits even to Spee's boldness: He published his book anonymously.)

Spee was not alone. A list of some of the other dissenters who published against the witch hunt before and after him reads like a roll call of nations: Samuel de Cassini of Italy in 1505; Johan Weyer, Germany, 1563; Alonzo Salazar de Frias, Spain, 1611; Gabriel Naudé, France, 1625; Balthasar Bekker, the Netherlands, 1691; and Robert Calef, England, 1700.

Among the dissenters was a German named Hermann Löher, who served as a law court official at Rheinbach, near Bonn, through two major witch hunts, in 1631 and 1636. The toll was high. On average, every other family lost at least one person. His experiences convinced him that innocent people had been tortured and killed in the witch courts and that victims under torture would confess to anything.

The Madness Crosses the Atlantic

The witchcraft hysteria came late to America. Although there were isolated witch trials throughout the colonies in the late 1600s, the phenomenon paled in comparison to the mass persecutions in Europe—until 1692, when a wave of witch madness engulfed the Massachusetts settlement of Salem. Before the year's end, nineteen men and women had been hanged and more than a hundred others arrested on charges of witchcraft.

For the people of Salem—as for most seventeenth-century New Englanders —witches and demons existed as surely as did the rocky land from which they scratched a living. Ruling this invisible world, as theologians of the time called it, was Satan himself. Odd incidents or coincidences and unaccountable illnesses were often attributed to the devil and his followers.

So when the village physician, Dr. Griggs, could find no physical cause for the "strange and unusual" behavior exhibited by two local children in the early months of 1692, he suspected they might be under Satan's spell. What else could explain why Puritan children, taught to be quiet and obedient, would suffer convulsive fits and scream blasphemies as the Reverend Samuel Parris's nine-year-old daughter, Elizabeth, and her eleven-year-old cousin, Abigail Williams, were doing?

The probable real cause of the girls' bizarre behavior was to be found in the Reverend Mr. Parris's own kitchen. There, unbeknown to him, his West Indian slave woman, Tituba, regularly regaled a group of enthralled girls with vivid tales of voodoo spells and witchcraft. Some of the girls, aided by Tituba, had even tried their hand at fortunetelling. But when the horrified Parris learned of these activities, the revelation only served to confirm his darkest suspicions and the doctor's diagnosis: The two children were victims not of illness but of witchcraft.

In a short time, several other girls and young women in the village began displaying even more dramatic symptoms, clutching their necks as if chok-

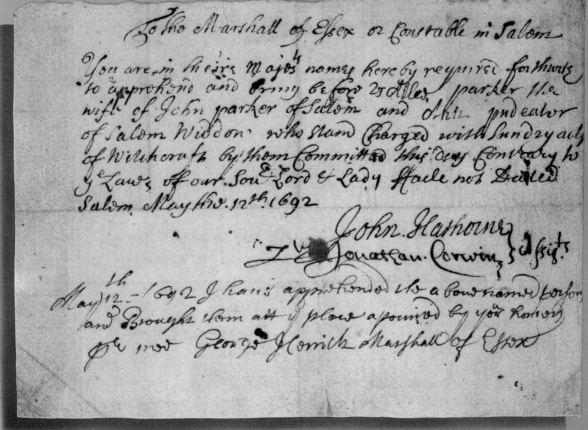

This handwritten arrest warrant charged Salem widow Ann Pudeator
"with sundry acts of witchcraft." After protesting that the evidence given against her
was "altogether false and untrue," Pudeator was hanged on September 22, 1692.

ing, twisting their bodies into contorted positions, and claiming temporary loss of speech, sight, and hearing. The girls also said they experienced spells in which a specter—or the likeness of a witch—bit, pinched, pricked, or otherwise tormented them.

Alarmed that Satan's servants appeared to be operating in their midst, a group of village leaders questioned the girls. Under mounting pressure, they named three women as witches— Sarah Good and Sarah Osborne, both unpopular villagers, and the slave Tituba. Brought before the local magistrates, Good and Osborne righteously declared their innocence. Tituba, however, confessed with gusto to all manner of witchcraft and traffic with the devil. Her enthusiastic testimony confirmed the villagers' worst fears of a demonic conspiracy. The three women were jailed to await formal trial.

Meanwhile, the girls warmed to their game and accused more people of witchcraft—men as well as women, the rich and respectable as well as the poor and despised. Salem plunged headlong into witch hysteria. Suspicion and fear thrived, and like an epidemic, the accusations and arrests spread to nearby settlements.

The witchcraft hearings began in May, when the colony's governor, Sir William Phips, set up a special court of oyer and terminer ("to hear and determine"). Ironically, the most incontrovertible type of evidence—a direct confession of witchcraft, such as Tituba's—was the one that virtually ensured the court's leniency. The self-declared guilty were forgiven and spared punishment, while those who refused to admit their transgressions were hanged. Thus the temptation to confess was great, and many of the accused took this route in order to save their lives. Others were persuaded to confess by tortures such as enforced sleeplessness or the binding of their necks and heels under increasing pressure until blood gushed from their noses.

If a reputed witch nonetheless con-

Replete with accusing fingers and swooning victims, T. H. Matteson's 1855 painting, The Trial of George Jacobs, depicts the chaos of the Salem courts. Jacobs's indicters included his own granddaughter, who later confessed that she testified only because the other girls blackmailed her.

tinued to plead innocent, the judges sought other forms of evidence, such as telltale witch's marks. Supplying the court with its most decisive evidence, however—and transforming the proceedings into a near circus—were the afflicted girls. Their hysterical reactions as the judges questioned an accused witch were deemed valid proof of the defendant's guilt. All too typical were their actions during Martha Cory's trial. "When she wrung her hands," read one account, "they screamed that they were being pinched; when she bit her lips, they declared that they could feel teeth biting their own flesh." Even more damning was so-called spectral evidence, based on one girl's claim that an apparition of the accused had tormented her. On such questionable grounds, six men and thirteen women, Sarah Good among them, were hanged. Two other condemned witches, including Sarah Osborne, died in jail. And Giles Cory, Martha Cory's husband, was slowly crushed to death for refusing to plead either guilty or not guilty.

How the Salem witch trials ever reached such a violent pitch is still debated today. Certainly the belief of the villagers and the judges in a malevolent invisible world provided a receptive atmosphere for the girls' accusations. The court's reliance on such dubious proof as spectral evidence, however, is—and was even then—less easily justified.

Central to the whole affair, of course, were the girls. The fits of little Elizabeth Parris and Abigail Williams are thought by many to have been rooted in vivid, emotionally exciting fantasies provoked by Tituba's dark tales. The older girls may then have emulated the hysterics to gain attention themselves. Or perhaps the group was simply being mischievous, playing a childish prank that quickly spun out of control. The girls may have been loath to shame themselves by admitting the truth and perhaps were intoxicated by their unaccustomed power.

There is some evidence that a play-

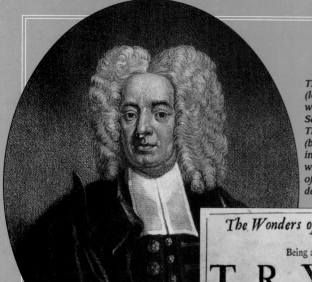

acting conspiracy of sorts existed. When twenty-year-old Mary Warren tried to retract her accusations, for instance, the other girls declared her to be a witch. Soon Mary was having fits and accusing others again. Some historians think the girls could have suffered true physical symptoms brought on by a hysterical, near-contagious reaction to the suggestion of bewitchment.

In such a suggestible state, the girls were probably easily influenced by the expectations of others; they probably implicated people based on negative impressions gleaned from adults. Moreover, the judges were not above proposing names to the girls, who more often than not confirmed their suggestions. Adult villagers joined in supporting the accusations, sometimes motivated by property squabbles or longstanding animosities.

Finally, one or two of the alleged witches may indeed have practiced the magic that everyone feared. Tituba's familiarity with West Indian voodoo and her immediate confession to witchcraft seemed to support that theory. And not only did tavern keeper Bridget Bishop's own husband accuse her of practicing the black arts, two laborers testified that they had found several needle-stuck rag dolls in her cellar wall.

Fortunately, by summer's end the public had become horrified by the death toll. In addition, local ministers had banded together to condemn the use of spectral evidence in the trials. One of the province's most respected clergymen, the Reverend Increase Mather, published a sermon signed by fourteen other pastors in which he said "it is better a guilty person should be absolved than that he should without ground of conviction be condemned." That fall Governor Phips forbade any more arrests and dismissed the court of oyer and terminer; the following spring the rest of the accused were acquitted or granted reprieves. Almost as suddenly as it had begun, the Salem witch mania had ended.

In this 1853 Matteson painting, Examination of a Witch, a humiliated suspect is searched for witch's marks. Cotton Mather approved the test, saying that he had never seen such marks, but "it is doubtless not impossible for a surgeon, when he sees them, to say what are magical."

His opposition to the trials put his life and the lives of his family in jeopardy, so he sold most of his property and fled to Amsterdam in 1636.

Forty years later he published a book entitled *Most Pressing Humble Complaint of the Pious Innocents,* in which he described in scathing terms how one judge conducted a witch trial. The judge rants at the defendant cowering before him: "You apostate, you witch, you dumb dog! Confess your sin of witchery; reveal the names of your accomplices! You filthy whore, you devil's wanton, you sackcloth-maker, you dumb toad! Speak and confess in God's name! Swallow the holy salt! Drink the holy water! Tell who it was that taught you witchcraft, and whom you saw and recognized at the witches' sabbat. Then you will not be tortured any more but have eternal life."

Speaking for himself, Löher wrote that "the early Christian martyrs were falsely accused of grievous crimes; but in our day, Christian witches are far more unjustly accused of mortal sins that they have not committed—and that they could not possibly commit." Löher fervently urged local princes in Germany to examine the court records, to reduce the appalling fees levied against the hapless victims, and most important, to halt the torture.

In England, where the witch mania was never as severe as on the Continent, and death by hanging the strictest, albeit the most tragic, punishment a witch might face, a healthy skepticism had long been evident. As early as 1582, a Kentish squire by the name of Reginald Scot, whose passion in life was the growing of hops, was shocked by the hanging of two luckless women at St. Osyth. They had been convicted of casting spells and consorting with familiars based on the testimony of some overwrought children, aged six through nine. Scot was moved to write *Discovery of Witches,* published in 1584, in which he attacked the very notion of witchcraft as a monstrous delusion. "What abominable and devilish inventions, and what flat and plain knavery is practiced against these old women," he declared.

But not everyone in England was so rational. Sporadic outbursts of witch-baiting occurred there every few years throughout the next century. The nation's most notorious witch hunter was an East Anglia lawyer of mediocre skills named Matthew Hopkins, who realized that he could make a better living by preying on the credulity of local farm communities. He would offer to track down neighborhood witches by using various practical tests, torture being prohibited by English law. One of his favorite methods of verification was "swimming," in which a suspect was trussed up and dunked into a convenient pond. If she floated it meant that the water rejected her, and she was a witch; if she sank she was innocent. Since this treatment

Basing his expertise on the hundreds he had condemned to burn, French prosecutor Nicholas Remy printed his own witches' handbook in 1595. A jumbled tome with a lurid emphasis on witches' sex lives, his Demonolatreiae rivaled the authority of the Malleus Maleficarum.

could easily result in drowning, the suspect stood to lose either way. Another test favored by Hopkins was to stick a suspect with pins, on the theory that any spot insensitive to pain was a devil's mark. For these attentions Hopkins charged a healthy fee.

Although Hopkins's career as a witch finder lasted little more than a year, from March 1645 to late spring of 1646, in that brief time he was responsible for the hanging of perhaps several hundred harmless old women and other alleged witches. Trials were held throughout the East of England—at Chelmsford, long thought to be a hotbed of witchcraft, at Huntingdon and Bury St. Edmonds, and in Norfolk. Often the most telling witnesses were undisciplined youngsters with overactive imaginations, who had been nurtured on ghost stories and fairy tales. But wiser heads soon prevailed, and Hopkins was forced into retirement.

By this time, the witch mania was abating throughout Europe. Businessmen and rulers viewed it as damaging to the economy. Intellectuals perceived it as irrational and inconsistent with the new scientific attitude that one day would cause the era now dawning to be called the Age of Enlightenment. By the century's turn, the rampant executions had ended in both France and Germany. In Spain, which had seen some witch burnings in Navarre and other northern provinces, the Inquisition had long since turned its attention to the pursuit of Jews, Moors, and other heretics. There was a sudden outbreak of witch-hunting in Sweden in 1669, at Mora, where eighty-five elderly women were put to death at the stake after a number of hysterical children claimed to have flown with them to sabbats. But that was the end of the terror in Scandinavia.

The last convicted English witches died in 1682, three mistreated elderly women who wearily climbed the gallows steps at Exeter.

Playing on the religious anxieties of a war-weary populace in the 1640s, Matthew Hopkins, England's self-appointed "witch finder general," caused more people to be hanged there for witchcraft in two years than in the whole previous century. Among the methods he used to wrest confessions from his victims were starvation and sleep deprivation.

After a lengthy trial at Lyons, Father Louis Debaraz was burned alive in 1745, accused of saying masses to the devil in hopes of locating hidden treasure; he was the last person to die as a convicted witch in France. The last German trial, in Swabia in 1775, resulted in the execution of one Anna Maria Schwagel. After that, no further death sentences were handed down for witchcraft. The great witch hunt was over—at least officially.

But even though church and state gave up the pursuit, the fear and loathing that those institutions had diligently cultivated for centuries was not immediately eradicated. Long after the last of the trials, reports of attacks on supposed witches popped up now and again from rural backwaters throughout Europe, places where people still clung to the old beliefs.

In 1875, in the village of Long Compton in Warwickshire, England, a poor and peaceable eighty-year-old woman, Anne Tennant, was viciously attacked and fatally wounded by a local farmhand armed with a pitchfork. "I meant to do it," declared her killer, a man named James Haywood. "There are several of them I will serve the same." It turned out that Haywood, who since childhood had been terrified of the whole notion of witches, was convinced some fifteen or sixteen of the night flyers were abroad in Long Compton and the surrounding countryside. A jury determined that he was insane.

His was not a totally isolated attitude, however. That same year near Newport, Wales, some miles to the west, a gang of workmen rudely accosted Margaret Grover, an aged woman long suspected of being a witch. Some in Newport laid every mishap and ill fortune at her doorstep. On this occasion, a little girl, Sarah Parvis, had died suddenly and inexplicably, and since Peg Grover had been in the neighborhood at the time, the child's death was attributed to her wicked ways. Seizing the old woman, the gang of men tied a rope around her waist. They ran one end of the rope over a tree limb, then hurled the unfortunate Peg Grover into a pond and with hoots of derision hauled on the rope to dunk her up and down—eight, ten, a dozen times. Gasping and coughing, the old woman was on the verge of drowning when some nearby residents came to her rescue.

Perhaps these and similar unsettling occurrences, some as recent as the twentieth century, are merely shudders from an already lifeless force, like the involuntary muscle spasms that continue after the death of an animal. That is certainly a preferable prospect to the alternative possibility the analogy suggests: that the witch-hunt beast is not dead but stirring in its sleep.

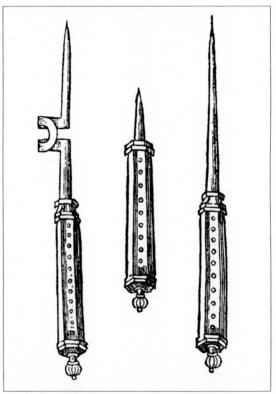

This drawing from a 1584 book by Englishman Reginald Scot reveals trick bodkins used to discover the callous devil's marks that labeled one a witch. A genuine bodkin appears at right above; the one at center had a retractable blade, and the notched tool at left only appeared to pierce the flesh.

Johan Weyer, physician to Duke William of Cleves, was among the first to denounce the excesses of witch hunters in Europe. Although he believed one could consort with the devil, Weyer wrote in 1563 that most witches were merely simple women unjustly accused. His views were extremely unpopular, and only his position with the duke prevented the doctor himself from suffering a convicted witch's fate.

Tools of the Torturer's Trade

rope's great witch hunt. Legal theory held that witches had to confess their guilt before they could be executed. But since witches would not willingly condemn themselves to death, torture was necessary to extract a confession. ''Not one witch in a million would be accused or punished if the procedure were governed by the ordinary rules,'' wrote a French witch-trial judge in 1580.

From the fifteenth century through the seventeenth, torturers expertly and ruthlessly wrenched confessions from hundreds of thousands of men, women, and children. As one woman convicted of witchcraft confessed to her priest before she died, ''I never dreamed that by

means of the torture a person could be brought to the point of telling such lies as I have told. I am not a witch, and I have never seen the devil, and still I had to plead guilty myself and denounce others.''

The origins of the devices the torturers employed, such as those pictured on these pages, are lost in history's murk. Most types were in use for centuries before the advent of witch trials. As far as is known, there were no large-scale manufacturers making the instruments. They were exceedingly durable, remaining in use for decades on end, and even during the witch-hunt era, local blacksmiths kept pace with the demand for replacements. Although some clearly were conceived by minds as brilliantly ingenious as they were sadistic, the identities of the inventors are not known; perhaps they stayed anonymous to avoid the dubious immortality that would come from having one's name eternally attached to such infernal implements.

Pain has been used as a test of truth since ancient times. Aristotle regarded torture as a sure means of gathering evidence and punishing wrongdoers, and works by the fifth-century-BC dramatist Aristophanes mention the employment of such grim devices as the rack and the wheel. During the heyday of the Roman Empire, detailed rules were imposed on the use of torture—soldiers, high-ranking nobility, and their descendants to the third generation were exempt, for example, as were children and pregnant women. But even these exemptions were waived when it came to sorcery.

Centuries later, religious zealots and secular authorities alike eagerly made torture the primary instrument of Eu-

In this 1532 woodcut, one torturer prepares to cut out a prisoner's tongue—a punishment for speaking blasphemy—while others flay their helpless victims with sticks and various scourges.

Torturers often applied bone-crushing vises, such as this spiked knee-splitter, to the arms, legs, or joints of accused witches. A Jesuit priest named Friedrich von Spee, an early-seventeenth-century opponent of the witch trials, pointed out that judges did not consider such devices torture, even though the prisoner's limbs "were pressed like a cake, bringing blood and causing intolerable pain."

Persons accused of desecrating the Sacrament—a frequent charge in witchcraft trials—often had their limbs severed by a hatchet (left). In Chamonix in 1642, for instance, Jean Gehauds was convicted of trampling on the Host; his foot was chopped off, then he was burned alive.

The metal-spiked, wooden interrogation chair was all the more sadistic for having a seat of iron that could be heated by a fire beneath it. The agony of searing metal piercing naked flesh proved unbearable; reportedly, few accused witches lasted more than fifteen minutes in the chair before making a full confession.

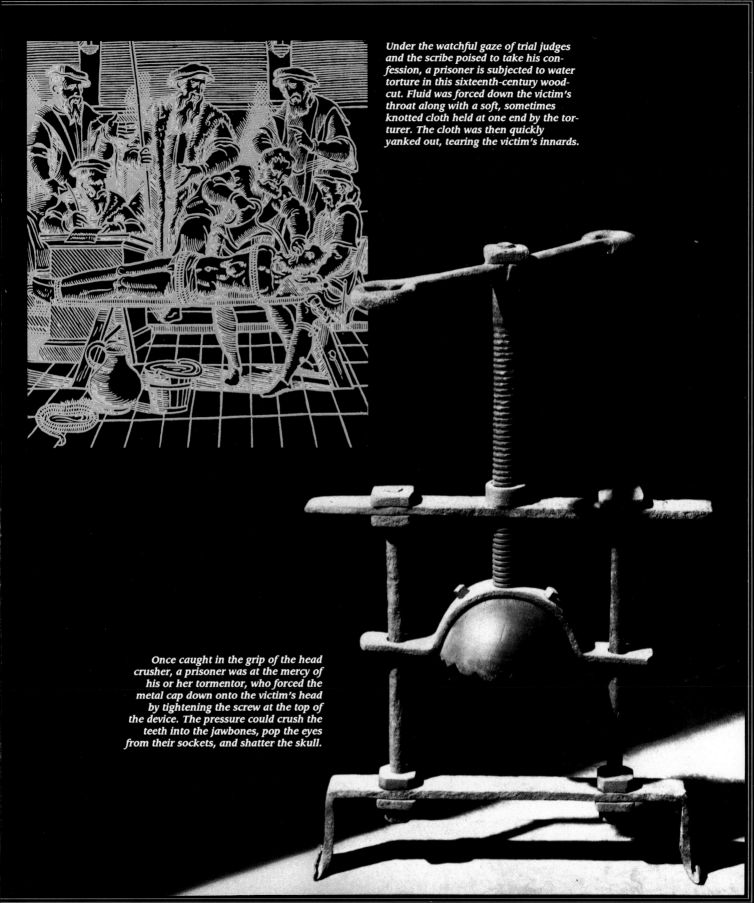

Under the watchful gaze of trial judges and the scribe poised to take his confession, a prisoner is subjected to water torture in this sixteenth-century woodcut. Fluid was forced down the victim's throat along with a soft, sometimes knotted cloth held at one end by the torturer. The cloth was then quickly yanked out, tearing the victim's innards.

Once caught in the grip of the head crusher, a prisoner was at the mercy of his or her tormentor, who forced the metal cap down onto the victim's head by tightening the screw at the top of the device. The pressure could crush the teeth into the jawbones, pop the eyes from their sockets, and shatter the skull.

Torturers crush a man by heaping hundreds of pounds of dead weight on him in this sixteenth-century woodcut. In England, pressing was used when defendants refused to enter a plea of guilty or not guilty. A plea was necessary before the accused could be tried, so some preferred to die from pressing rather than answer charges, thus saving their names from the taint of a witchcraft conviction.

Standard equipment in nearly every torture chamber was the rack. Accused witches were tied or strapped onto the table and their bodies stretched as much as twelve inches by force of the winch. First a victim's shoulders were dislocated; eventually, the knees, hips, and elbows were pulled from their sockets, and the muscles ripped from the limbs. This rack features a set of spiked rollers, a sadistic refinement that was more the exception than the rule.

The seemingly innocuous wheel
was used for one of the most
atrocious punishments meted
out to condemned witches.
As shown in the 1548 woodcut
above, victims were first
stretched spread-eagle on the
ground and tied to stakes. The
executioner then smashed every
major bone of the accused
with the heavy wheel, threaded
the mangled body through its
spokes, and hoisted it atop a
pole. Witches were burned after
being thus desecrated; other
criminals were left to the crows.

A Condemned Man's Testament

Many hundred thousand good-nights, dearly beloved daughter Veronica. Innocent have I come into prison, innocent have I been tortured, innocent must I die.'' With these words of resignation to a grotesque and undeserved fate, Johannes Junius, a burgomaster, or chief magistrate, of the city of Bamberg—situated in a tiny principality of the same name—began a letter of farewell to his daughter. The writing was arduous, because the prisoner's hands were mutilated by the thumbscrews that had been used to coerce his confession. But the words that he scrawled were both proud and poignant.

Junius's sense of his own righteousness was almost all that was left to him. When he wrote the farewell letter to his daughter on July 24, 1628, he was already beyond any hope of proving his innocence. ''For whoever comes into the witch prison,'' the burgomaster de-

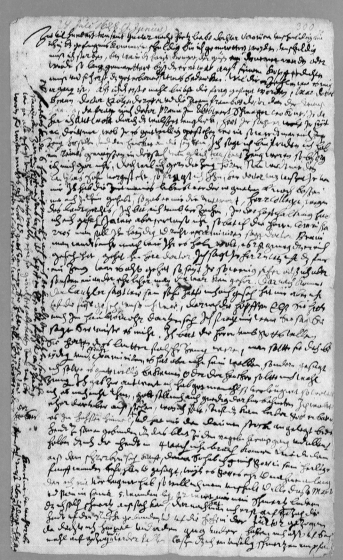

Wracked by torture and barely able to grasp his quill pen, Johannes Junius (opposite) writes to his daughter from prison. His letter (right) provides a rare personal account of the experience of being tried as a witch.

clared, "must become a witch or be tortured until he invents something out of his head."

In the course of the witch persecutions that peaked in the seventeenth century, thousands of innocent Europeans suffered the same ignominious end that befell Junius. The burgomaster's wife had been incinerated in the witch oven—a crematorium located in the nearby town of Zeil—only months earlier. In Bamberg as in some other regions, witch-hunting had become a form of state-controlled crime that was complete with its own bureaucracy; the entire apparatus was used by rulers to steal the wealth of the victims. Unlike most of the accused witches, Junius had the opportunity to leave behind a personal testimony to his suffering, to the nightmarish farce of his trial, and to the calculated ruthlessness of his inquisitors.

Junius was able to smuggle the letter out of prison with the assistance of one of his guards. The communication carried specific instructions for his daughter to pay the jailer one thaler—a silver coin—as a means of compensating the man for his troubles. Junius admonished his daughter to hide the document, "else I shall be tortured most piteously and the jailers will be beheaded." He further instructed her to save herself by fleeing the city of Bamberg immediately. The young woman did manage to escape; whether or not she ever received her father's letter, however, is nowhere recorded.

Even for those times, the Bamberg of Johannes Junius was notorious for the scope and brutality of its witch trials. Beginning in 1595, inquisitors systematically tortured and executed hundreds of townspeople, including many of the principality's leading citizens, all on trumped-up charges. Prince-Bishop Johann Georg II, Fuchs von Dornheim, who served as the independent ruler of Bamberg, presided over the worst of the atrocities, which occurred during the 1620s. With the assistance of an ecclesiastical administrator as well as a full-time staff of lawyers, torturers, and

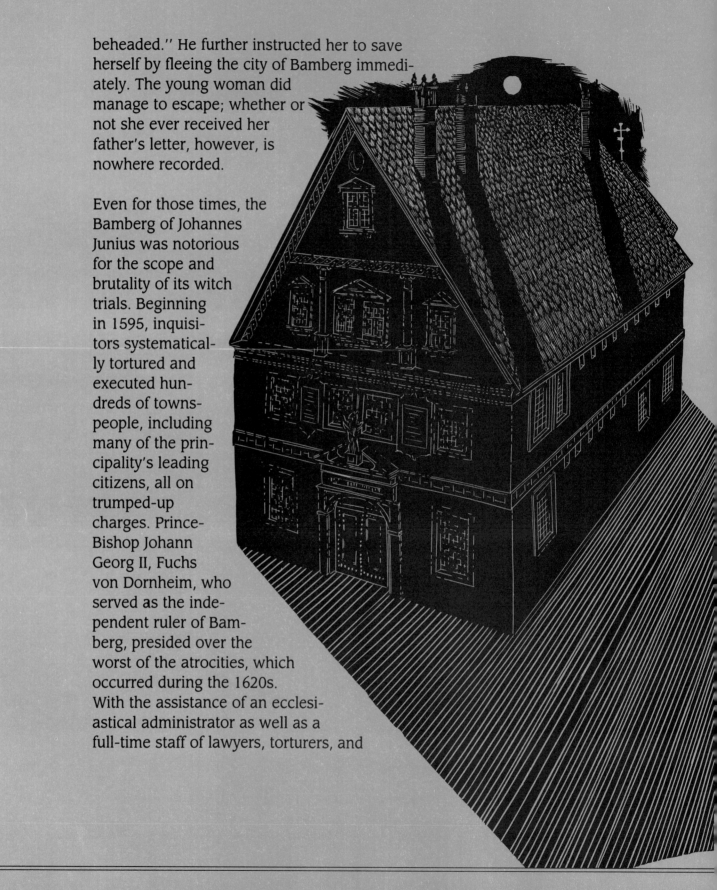

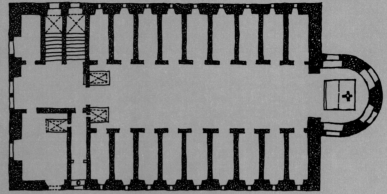

The infamous Trudenhaus (left) was constructed in Bamberg as a prison for accused witches. The building's attractive exterior contrasted sharply with the atrocities that occurred within. A floor plan (right) shows cells lining a central hall, a confession room next to the stairway, and a chapel in an alcove at the far end of the hall.

executioners, Johann Georg sent no fewer than 600 citizens to their deaths. Furthermore, he ordered the construction of a special prison called the Trudenhaus, or witch house, a facility to hold those who were awaiting trial.

The prince-bishop confiscated the property of everyone who was convicted of witchcraft. By all accounts, Johann Georg saw to it that his witch hunters made the most of this extraordinary arrangement. A list that was compiled shortly after the persecutions ceased in 1631 indicates that the prince-bishop's henchmen had confiscated some 500,000 florins—or gold coins—from the victims they had executed and they had taken another 220,000 florins from suspects that were still locked up in prison.

In addition to the profit motive, there was another incentive for the merciless destruction of alleged witches in Bamberg. In a religiously divided Germany, which had been wracked by the devastations of the Thirty Years' War, Catholic and Protestant armies frequently engaged in regional skirmishes. Catholic rulers such as Johann Georg used witchcraft as a pretense for rooting out the opposition Lutherans in their dominions.

In an effort to justify their actions, these leaders cited religious arguments formulated by Jesuit and Dominican theologians. The aim of the clerics in producing these writings had less to do with clarifying religious doctrine than it did with winning back the Protestant strongholds in Germany. Protestant authorities responded in kind, conducting their own witch hunts.

Thumbscrews and leg vises were used in the early stages of an increasingly terrible sequence of tortures. Junius's resolve held firm as his fingers were mashed to a pulp, but it yielded under the force of more brutal treatment (opposite).

Church support notwithstanding, the severity of the Bamberg trials eventually evoked revulsion among the townspeople. In 1630 and 1631, Johann Georg's titular overlord, the Holy Roman Emperor Ferdinand II, finally ordered reforms. His most important stipulation was to put an end to the confiscation of the victims' property. Without the prospect of spoils—and threatened by an advancing Protestant army—the prince-bishop began to lose enthusiasm. Executions eventually ceased in 1631, and within another year the tyrannical Johann Georg had died of natural causes.

Ferdinand's reforms and the demise of the prince-bishop came too late, unfortunately, to save the life of Johannes Junius. Perhaps more than anything, his letter from prison captures the ruthlessness of the men who profited from the business of executing alleged witches. Among those who conducted Junius's trial was his own brother-in-law, a man by the name of Dr. Braun.

"I will tell you how it has gone with me," Junius wrote. "When I was the first time put to the torture, my brother-in-law Dr. Braun, Dr. Köthendörffer, and two strange doctors were there. Then Dr. Braun asks me, 'Kinsman, how come you here?' I answered, 'Through falsehood and misfortune.' 'Hear, you,' he retorts, 'you are a witch. Will you confess it voluntarily? If not, we'll bring in witnesses and the executioner for you.' I said, 'I am no witch; I have a pure conscience in the matter.' "

The tribunal then confronted Junius with a number of witnesses, each one of them a confessed witch, who, after being subjected to various means of torture, had identified Bamberg's burgomaster as a willing

Junius drops in agony as his tormentors subject him to the strappado. Suspended from his wrists, which were bound behind him, he was hoisted up on a pulley and dropped nearly to the floor eight times, thereby dislocating his shoulders.

participant in their rituals. When the chief magistrate refused to confirm the accusations, his suffering began in earnest: "And then came alas—God in highest heaven have mercy—the executioner, and put the thumbscrews on me, both hands bound together, so that the blood spurted from the nails and everywhere, so that for four weeks I could not use my hands, as you can see from my writing.

"Thereafter they stripped me, bound my hands behind me, and drew me up on the pulley. Then I thought heaven and earth were at an end. Eight times did they draw me up and let me fall again, so that I suffered terrible agony. . . .

"And this happened on Friday, June 30, and with God's help I had to bear the torture. When at last the executioner led me back into the cell, he said to me, 'Sir, I beg you, for God's sake, confess something, whether it be true or not. Invent something, for you cannot endure the torture which you will be put to; and, even if you bear it all, yet you will not escape.' "

This advice, as well as indications from the tribunal that the prince-bishop wished to make an example of him, convinced Junius that he had no choice but to fabricate a confession. He stated that he had been seduced by a demon in female form called a succubus, had denounced God and sworn fealty to the devil, and like a witch had ridden off to sabbat ceremonies on a flying black dog.

"Then I had to tell what crimes I had committed. I said nothing. . . . 'Hoist the knave up!' So I said that I was to kill my children, but I had killed a horse instead. It did not help. I had also taken a sacred wafer, and had buried it. When I said this, they left me in peace."

But the witch hunters were not quite through with Junius. Later they demanded that he name accomplices. They grilled him with such pointed questions that he could easily guess the names that they wanted to hear. With regrets, the burgomaster gave them the false information they sought.

"Now, my dearest child," he wrote Veronica, "here you have all my acts and confession, for which I must die. And it is all sheer lies and inventions, so help me God." In a postscript he added that in prison the six witnesses against him had begged his forgiveness before they were executed, saying they had accused him to save themselves from more torture, just as he had accused others for the same reason.

The closing words of the burgomaster's letter were filled with despair: "Good night, for your father Johannes Junius will never see you more."

The end came for Johannes Junius in a relatively quick and merciful fashion—he was beheaded with a sword while sitting in a chair. Although he was not burned alive like many of those convicted of the same crimes, Junius did not escape the flames entirely. His broken body was transported to the village of Zeil for cremation in the witch oven.

CHAPTER 3

Witchcraft Today

arishioners of Boston's venerable Arlington Street Church have seen and heard many things over the years. After all, in this sanctuary the Unitarian gospel of a singular, not a threefold, God rumbled down over generations of worshipers. Here, too, in an earlier age of crisis, the abolitionist William Ellery Channing railed against the evils of slavery. And in this same church, a century later, opponents of the American venture in Vietnam rallied in protest of that conflict.

It is fair to imagine, however, that even such adventurous church members could hardly have conjured the improbable scene that occurred on an April Friday in 1976. That evening, as church lights dimmed and the riffle of a flute slid over the heads of more than a thousand gathered women, four witches, each one bearing a single candle, took places around the altar. At the chancel with them stood a high priestess of witchcraft, Morgan McFarland, herself the daughter of a Protestant minister. In a clear and steady voice, McFarland began a long and mystical-sounding incantation that was a far cry indeed from any doctrine that Unitarian parishioners would have recognized: "In the infinite moment before all Time began, the Goddess arose from Chaos and gave birth to Herself . . . before anything else had been born . . . not even Herself. And when She had separated the Skies from the Waters and had danced upon them, the Goddess in Her ecstasy created everything that is. Her movements made the wind, and the Element Air was born and did breathe."

As the high priestess continued to chant in this manner, describing her own version of creation, her colleagues at the altar began to light candles in turn—first to the east, then south, then west, and finally north. McFarland's voice rang out, sounding for all the world like an ancient seeress, calling upon the great female deity who, the priestess declared, had created both the heavens and the earth. At the culmination of her chant, McFarland recalled how the goddess had made the first women and taught them the names that were to be used ever after in prayer: "I am Artemis, Maiden of the Animals, Virgin of the Hunt. I am Isis, the Great Mother. I am Ngame, the Ancient One who winds the shroud. And I shall be called a million names.

Call unto me, daughters, and know that I am Nemesis."

The occasion was a three-day conference on women's spirituality, and this ceremony, despite such familiar elements as candles, robes, and music, was as unorthodox an opening prayer as had ever echoed within the brownstone walls of the Arlington Street Church. It was also infectious, and by its end many in the audience were dancing in the aisles, and a thousand voices filled the stately old church with a single chant: "The Goddess is alive, magic is afoot. The Goddess is alive, magic is afoot."

To many scholars who have studied the history of witchcraft, the goddess being invoked at the ceremony—whose ecstatic dance is said to have woven wind and air and fire, and whose laughter, it is claimed, blew life into all women—could not have been around for the creation at all, because she was born and given form as well as character in some strictly modern imaginations. Her historical provenance, the skeptics say, is limited to a few traits culled from cloudy notions of the deities of pre-Christian Europe, now overlaid with theatrical details that have been consciously devised to suit ceremonial needs.

But for many modern practitioners of witchcraft, their Great Goddess is indeed an ancient creator spirit who was worshiped in Europe and the Near East long before the Christian God was introduced there. They believe she survived centuries of persecution by hiding in the hearts of her secret adherents, spiritual daughters and sons who went to the rack and stake of the Inquisition because of their beliefs. And now, they say, the goddess moves abroad once more, openly, stirring celebrations in strongholds of the very same organized religion that once attempted to expunge every trace of her and her followers.

Her followers today do not express any doubts about the antiquity of their faith. To be a witch, says one, is "to put yourself into close consonance with some ways that are older than the human race itself." Indeed, even some non-initiates claim that they perceive in the witchcraft move-

ment an unseen force animating the universe. One woman, who wrote off the teachings and trappings of witchcraft as little more than "just words, meaningless in themselves," said that she nevertheless sensed a force that seemed to be hovering outside of reason's reach when she was in a place where witches gather. "I feel a current," she confided in a letter to a friend, "a force that surrounds us. It's alive, it pulsates, it ebbs and flows like the waxing and waning of the moon . . . I don't know what it is, and I don't know how to use it. It's like being near an electric current, very near, so near you can hear it humming and crackling, but not being able to tap into it."

Today, however, thousands of otherwise ordinary men and women believe they are tapping into this current and drawing on what author Theodore Roszak calls the "wellspring of human spiritual consciousness." In the process, these self-proclaimed neopagans are discovering—or as some of them put it, rediscovering—what they say is an age-old religion, one whose language is the language of myth and ritual, whose faith is as real as rapture and as difficult to define, and whose god is not one but many. These modern-day nature worshipers, like pagans of earlier eras, do not sift the natural from the supernatural, the ordinary from the extraordinary, the mundane from the spiritual. To a neopagan, all are one and the same.

Estimates of the number of neopagans run as high as 100,000 or more in the United States, a membership that is reflected in the veritable explosion of pagan festivals since the 1970s. In the late 1980s, there were more than fifty such festivals in the United States, together attracting people from the deeply committed to the merely curious. According to Margot Adler, author of *Drawing Down the Moon,* a book that documents the rise of neopaganism, these festivals "have completely changed the face of the pagan movement" and are creating a national pagan community. Adler claims that this group comprises a cross section of society, including tatooists and tugboat captains as well as bankers, lawyers, and librarians, and a large number of computer professionals.

Not all of today's neopagans can be called witches, however, since not all of them wrap the neopagan worship of nature and ancient deities in the trappings of ritual magic, as witches do. But an unknown number of neopagans do subscribe to the tenets of a faith that is popularly called witchcraft and is known to the initiated as the craft. The religion is also known by the name of Wicca, an Old English word for a male witch; the term may also be related to the Indo-European roots *wic* and *weik,* meaning "to bend" or "to turn." Hence, in the eyes of modern Wiccans, witches were never the hags or seductresses that the populace purported them to be but those women and men who could bend reality by means of magic. Wiccans believe that the witches of history were the village healers and the local fonts of traditional lore and wisdom. As such, they were also the pillars of peasant society.

But stereotypes persist, and witches continue to be the objects of calumny, struggling to shed their notoriety and their image as the consorts of the devil. To many people, a witch was—and still is—a devil worshiper. Even as recently as 1952, the British author Pennethorne Hughes branded some historical witches as "dissipated perverts" and listed a host of real or imagined sins. "Witches cast spells," he wrote, "they raised havoc, they poisoned, they aborted cattle and inhibited human beings, they served the Devil, parodied Christian practices, allied themselves with the King's enemies, they copulated with other witches in male and female form whom they took to be incubi or succubi, they committed abuses with domestic animals."

Under such an indictment, it is not at all surprising that the words *witch* and *witchcraft* continue to arouse revulsion. "Witchcraft is a word that frightens many people and confuses many others," observes a California-based writer and witch who goes by the name Starhawk. "In the popular imagination," she notes, witches of the past are "ugly old hags riding broomsticks, or evil Satanists performing obscene rites." And modern-day opinion has not shown any more kindness toward modern-day witches, holding them to be, Starhawk points out, "members of a kooky cult, which lacks the depth, dignity and seriousness of purpose of true religion."

But a religion it is, both in the eyes of those witches who describe religion as "a human need for beauty," and when measured against the dictionary's definition of religion as an "institutionalized system of religious attitudes, beliefs and practices." Even the U.S. Department of Defense

---

MURDER FARMER TO GET LOCK OF HAIR TO BREAK SPELL, THREE CONFESS

Nelson D. Rehmeyer, North Hopewell Township Farmer, Slain By Wilbert Hess, 18 Years, John Blymyer 32, And John Curry, 14, When He Refuses To Be Shorn Of Locks Which Assailants Wanted To Bury Under Eight Feet Of Ground

SET FIRE TO BODY TO HIDE TRACES OF CRIME

Braying Of Mule Leads To Discovery Of Slain Man In His Lonel⋯ Four⋯

District Attorney Collap⋯ M⋯

Despite the modern popularity of witchcraft as a religion, the medieval belief that witches can wield evil powers has never completely vanished. It was still strong enough in 1928 in York County, Pennsylvania, to have deadly results. Two men and a boy confessed to killing Nelson Rehmeyer, a reclusive farmer and self-proclaimed witch, to get a lock of his hair. They needed it, they said, to break the spells he had cast on them. John Blymyer, eldest of the three, declared that he, too, was a witch and that for fifteen years he had sought the person to blame for his misfortunes. He said soon after his arrest, "Rehmeyer is dead. I no longer feel bewitched. Now I can sleep and eat."

Blymyer and his friends were not alone in their beliefs. Newspapers told of others who tried to break spells; a barber reported that some customers took their hair clippings with them, as a way to avert "severe headaches." After the York County coroner lamented that half the county believed in the black arts, local medical societies announced a "crusade against the practice of witchcraft and its allied evil creeds."

has given its imprimatur to Wicca's claims of being a valid religion, and in the mid-1970s, the Pentagon recruited a witch called Lady Theos to revise the chapter on witchcraft in the official U.S. Army chaplains' handbook. Lady Theos's contributions were updated in 1985 by a high-profile neo-pagan named Selena Fox. Another sign of the times can be read on the dog tags worn by members of the armed forces for identification, where the words *pagan* and *Wiccan* now appear as routinely—though certainly not as frequently—as do the names of other religious affiliations.

In spite of this recognition and in spite of the constitutional guarantee of freedom of worship, the practice of witchcraft still meets with harsh criticism and even purposeful persecution. These assaults do not compare in scale or in savagery, of course, with the prolonged reign of terror from the fourteenth through the seventeenth centuries that contemporary witches refer to as the Burning Time, or the Great Witch Hunt. In fact, this current persecution is benign by comparison: unwarranted dismissals from jobs, loss of custody of children, nuisance arrests, vandalism—quiet but damaging torments that have prompted Wiccan high priest-

This 1602 copy of the Malleus Maleficarum, the medieval witch-hunter's guide, is a link with the past for its owner, Andras Corban Arthen, a Wiccan high priest in Boston. The Malleus directed inquisitors to secure confessions by means of torture. This copy is allegedly bound in the skin of a witch.

ess Morgan McFarland to label the present era as a "subtle Burning Time."

The source of at least some of today's comparative tolerance, as well as the roots of the Wiccan revival, can be found in the work done early in the twentieth century by Margaret Murray, a British anthropologist. Murray's research into the origins and history of witchcraft began, as she later recalled in her autobiography, with "the usual idea that the Witches were all old women suffering from illusions about the Devil." But following the paper trail of trial documents left behind by the Inquisition, Murray soon unmasked the devil, she said, and discovered instead what she identified as the horned male god of an organized fertility cult, a pagan deity whom the inquisitors—in their search for religious heresy—had twisted into a convenient embodiment of evil. Further study of the records convinced her that this god also had a female form—a medieval version of the divine huntress of classical times, who had been called Artemis by the Greeks and Diana by the Romans. Murray alleged that the doomed witches came to revere Diana as their spiritual leader.

As Murray came to regard it, witchcraft and the pre-Christian fertility religion she would christen the Dianic cult were not only one and the same but also appeared to be "the ancient religion of Western Europe." This faith, she theorized, could be traced back some 25,000 years to an aboriginal race that was made up of dwarfs, whose existence was recorded by the conquering invaders only in superstitious tales of elves and fairies. It was this "joyous religion," as Murray described it, with its feasting, dancing, and sexual abandon, that was so incomprehensible to the gloomy inquisitors that their only recourse was to torch it to its very roots.

In 1921, Murray aired her findings in *The Witch Cult in*

Much-publicized witch Selena Fox greets the world from Spirit Rock, a Wisconsin prominence that is part of what she calls the sacred pagan land of her Wiccan church, Circle Sanctuary. "I was guided to this land in a dream," Fox said. "Communing with nature is at the heart of our spiritual practice."

Western Europe, the first of three books that she would publish on the subject and the one that was to lend a certain legitimacy to the Wiccan religion. Other scholars, however, immediately attacked both Murray's methods and her conclusions. One critic simply dismissed her book as "vapid balderdash." Although Margaret Murray's work has never carried much weight in academic circles, recent archaeological studies have induced a few historians to at least take a second, less dismissive, look at some of the author's more controversial theories. Even in her own day, moreover, Murray did manage, through her favorable reassessment of witchcraft, to throw open the door for a surge of interest in the Dianic cult.

Those who followed Murray's lead and ventured inside that door soon discovered that they were also dogging the trail of an American writer and folklorist named Charles Leland. In 1899, more than two decades before Murray propounded her theories, Leland had published *Aradia,* which he described as the gospel of *la Vecchia Religione,* or "the Old Religion," a phrase that has since found its way into Wiccan lore. Purportedly the translation of an Italian witch's secret manual of myths and spells, the book spins the tale of Diana, the Queen of Witches, whose tryst with the sun god Lucifer results in a daughter named Aradia. It is this Aradia, *la prima strega,* or "the first witch," who reveals the secrets of witchcraft to humanity.

At best unreliable and probably an outright fraud, *Aradia* has nevertheless provided the inspiration for a number of rites practiced by contemporary witches, including the Charge of the Goddess, an invocation that exhorts its listerners to "assemble in some secret place and adore the Spirit of Me, who am Queen of all the Witcheries." And although it has few if any scholarly defenders to oppose its detractors, *Aradia* has helped fan the flames of the current revival of witchcraft, and its emphasis on the worship of the goddess has made the book especially popular among the feminist covens.

A work with a similar bent, but of a sounder reputa-

tion and a later vintage, is Robert Graves's book, *The White Goddess,* which was first published in 1948. In its pages, Graves argued lyrically for the existence of an ancient cult centered on the worship of a matriarchal moon goddess. According to the author, this goddess was the only salvation for modern Western civilization and doubled as the muse who inspires all poetry. But if many of its early readers found in *The White Goddess* a rationale for witchcraft and if later Wiccans continued to see the book as a source of inspirational ideas, Graves himself expressed several reservations about the craft. His ambivalence is apparent in a 1964 essay in which the author took note of Wicca's longevity and its good health, on the one hand, but then called the craft to task for its emphasis on what Graves referred to as fun and games. What witchcraft really needed, wrote Graves, was for "some gifted mystic to come forward, reunite, and decently reclothe it, and restore its original hunger for wisdom."

Graves's reference was a scornful jab at a curiously charismatic elderly Englishman, Gerald Brosseau Gardner, who had exerted a major—but to Graves's mind, frivolous—influence on the resurgence of interest in witchcraft. Gardner, who was born in 1884 near Liverpool, had several careers, including British customs officer, rubber planter, anthropologist, and finally, self-proclaimed mystic. No slave to convention, he was an enthusiastic nudist, and he professed a lifelong interest in "magic and kindred subjects," which for him included everything from Britain's Little People to the Inquisition's victims, to the secret cults of ancient Greece, Rome, and Egypt. For a time he belonged to the famous society of would-be magicians called the Hermetic Order of the Golden Dawn.

Gerald Gardner rattled the doors of established scholarship when he announced that what Margaret Murray had theorized was true. Witchcraft, he said, had been a religion and in fact still was. Gardner declared that he knew because he was himself a witch. His startling pronouncement came in 1954 with the publication of *Witchcraft Today,* the book most responsible for the revival of witchcraft. Publication of this volume would have been impossible before 1951, when the rickety Witchcraft Acts of 1735 were finally repealed by the British Parliament. Interestingly, Parliament rescinded these ordinances under pressure from the Spiritualist churches, whose efforts to communicate with the spirits of the departed had also been curtailed by the laws. The repeal met with little opposition because lawmakers expected that surely after more than three centuries of persecution and another 200 years of silence, witchcraft had to be well and truly dead.

If the craft was not dead, as *Witchcraft Today* claimed to prove, Gardner himself did at least admit that it was dying when he first encountered it in 1939. It was Gardner's contention that after the calamity of the Burning Time, witchcraft had smoldered secretly through the ensuing centuries, while its canon of lore and ritual was passed from one generation of witches to another. Gardner's penchant for matters occult had led, he said, to a meeting with an heiress of this ancient tradition, "Old Dorothy" Clutterbuck, who was allegedly the high priestess of a surviving coven. Soon after this encounter, Gardner was initiated into the craft, although he later asserted—in the most improbable claim of

Egyptologist Margaret A. Murray, whose writings fueled the modern witchcraft revival, catches a remark with her ear trumpet. An active scholar until she died at 100 in 1963, Murray lived by the motto of Kipling's fictional mongoose, Rikki-Tikki Tavi: "Run and find out."

an unsubstantiated tale—that he remained in the dark about Old Dorothy's intentions until midway through the initiation ceremony, when he heard the word *Wicca* and realized "that that which I had thought burnt out hundreds of years ago still survived."

Considering himself duly anointed, Gardner gradually assumed the mantle of unofficial spokesperson for the craft. It was in this guise that he shed new light on the heretofore shadowy activities of witches, describing in *Witchcraft Today,* for example, the craft's alleged role in preventing Adolf Hitler's invasion of England. According to Gardner, the covens of Great Britain met on the coast of England in 1940, together raised the "burning brand"—an intense agglomeration of spiritual energy also known as the cone of power—and supposedly beamed a mental message to the führer: "You cannot come. You cannot cross the sea." Whether their magic spell had its desired effect or not is debatable, although, as

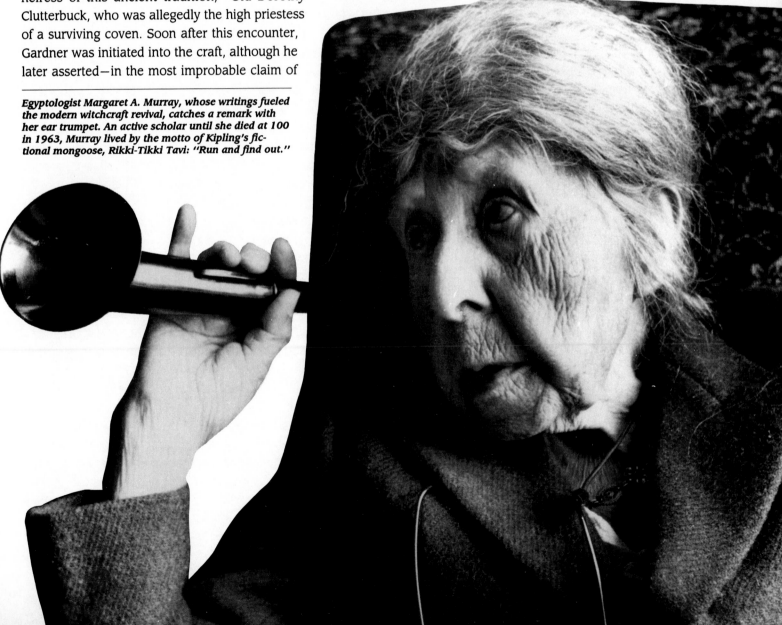

English poet Robert Graves inadvertently fueled the resurgence of witchcraft by imparting his vision of the primal female deity in his 1948 book, The White Goddess. Her worship, he said, though suppressed by the early Christian emperors, was preserved in the study of poetry, as well as in the covens of Western Europe.

Gardner himself was quick to point out, history does record that Hitler reconsidered his planned invasion of England at the last minute and abruptly set his sights on Russia instead. A similar burning brand, Gardner also claimed, apparently was the undoing of the Spanish Armada in 1588, when covens of witches conjured up a storm that swallowed the mightiest navy of its time.

When he was not rewriting history, Gerald Gardner took it upon himself to revise the practice of witchcraft. Drawing on his own considerable research into ritual magic, he concocted a literary witches' brew that was made up of fragments of ancient rituals supposedly preserved by his fellow coven members, as well as elements of Masonic rite and quotations from his friend and colleague Aleister Crowley, the renowned occultist and self-styled Great Beast of ritual magic. Gardner then decided to add a dash of Aradia and the White Goddess, and, for good measure, he incorporated a pinch each of Ovid and Rudyard Kipling. The end result, which was written in mock Elizabethan English and thickened by the addition of 162 so-called Craft Laws, was a kind of catechism for Gardner's resuscitated Wicca. No sooner was it completed than its compiler attempted to pass it off as a sixteenth-century witch's notebook, or a Book of Shadows.

Despite its questionable pedigree, the volume became both gospel and liturgy for the Gardnerian tradition of Wicca, as this latest incarnation of witchcraft came to be called. It was "a peaceful, happy nature religion," as Margot Adler depicts it in Drawing Down the Moon. "Witches met in covens, led by a priestess. They worshipped two principal deities, the god of forests and what lies beyond, and the great Triple Goddess of fertility and rebirth. They met in the nude in a nine-foot circle and raised power from their bodies through dancing and chanting and meditative techniques. They focused primarily on the Goddess; they celebrated the eight ancient pagan festivals of Europe and sought to attune themselves to nature."

As Gardner himself asked in Witchcraft Today, "Is there anything very wicked or awful in all this? If it were performed in a church, omitting the word goddess or substituting the name of a saint, would anyone object?"

Perhaps not, although the ritual nudity prescribed by Gardner would—and still does—raise eyebrows. But to Gardner, clothing merely impeded the release of the psychic power that he believes is pent up in the human body. By worshiping in the nude, witches not only shed their everyday attire but also, by extension, their everyday life. Moreover, their nudity represented a symbolic return to a time before the loss of innocence.

Gardner found justification for ritual nudity in his adaptation of Aradia's Charge of the Goddess, in which la prima strega instructs her followers that "as a sign that ye be truly free, ye shall be naked in your rites; and ye shall sing, feast, make music and love, all in my praise." The prescript nudity, added to Gardner's advocacy of ritual sex—the Great Rite, as he called it—virtually cried out for criticism. Before long, the father of the Gardnerian tradition was saddled with the reputation of dirty old man.

But as a lifelong nudist and occultist, Gardner was accustomed to society's sidelong glances, and in Witchcraft Today, he even seemed to anticipate the criticism he eventually got. He garnered little sympathy among his detractors, however, by choosing to characterize ritual nudity as "a family party trying a scientific experiment according to the textbook." Worse still for Gardner, some of his critics thought that they smelled fraud after examining his writings closely, and they began to question the validity of his supposedly timeworn Book of Shadows as well as his claim of an unbroken heritage for witchcraft.

Among the loudest of the discreditors was the historian Elliot Rose, whose 1962 critique dismissed Gardner's brand of witchcraft as syncretic and mockingly advised those seeking mystical profundity in witchcraft to choose any ten "moonstruck companions" and form a coven of their own. "It will be as traditional, as well-instructed, and as authentic as any there has been these thousand years," Rose noted acidly.

woman to the status of high priestess, the use of a circle to concentrate a coven's power, and even the ritual of Drawing Down the Moon, in which a high priestess temporarily "becomes" the goddess, were all Gardnerian contributions to the craft. Moreover, writing in a pagan journal in 1984, Kelly noted that there was absolutely no basis for Gardner's assertion that his tradition had its roots in the ancient pagan religion of Europe.

In the same article, Kelly provided details on the origins of Gardner's controversial Book of Shadows. The work got its start, Kelly surmised, not in the sixteenth century, as Gardner had claimed, but in the early years of the Second World War. Gardner had begun to keep a notebook, *Ye Bok of Ye Art Magical,* into which he copied various rituals that he had scavenged from other occult traditions, as well as favorite passages gleaned from his reading. By the time that first notebook was filled up, Kelly wrote, Gardner had all the makings of the very first Book of Shadows.

Kelly also drew attention to a profound revision that had come over Gardner's "tradition," showing it to be, not the faithful continuation of a religion rooted in the millennia, but a recent concoction and quite a changeable one at that. In its early years, Gardnerian Wicca had been focused on worship of the male side of the godhead, Kelly noted. By the mid-1950s, however, the Horned God had been eclipsed by the Great Goddess. A comparable change of command had taken place in the workings of the coven, where the high priest was suddenly playing second fiddle to a high priestess. As Kelly brought to light, these changes came about only after Doreen Valiente, who had been the first

Even-harsher critics held their fire until after 1964, when Gerald Gardner was safely stowed away in his grave. One, a prominent British chronicler of the occult named Francis King, accused Gardner of founding an "elaborate and romanticized witch-cult of his own," more or less out of boredom. King even went so far as to declare that Gardner had hired fellow magician Aleister Crowley to pen a new liturgy for him.

Another critic is Aidan Kelly, a founder of the New, Reformed, Orthodox Order of the Golden Dawn, a craft offshoot. Kelly stated matter-of-factly that Gardner invented modern witchcraft, that in a misguided attempt to reform the old religion, he formed an entirely new one. According to Kelly, the preeminence of the goddess, the elevation of a

Gardnerian high priestess, began adopting Robert Graves's White Goddess myth as the official system of beliefs about the goddess. In fact, Valiente is, in Kelly's view, the true author of most Gardnerian rituals.

Nevertheless, Kelly tempered his otherwise blistering criticism of Gardner by giving him credit not only for creative genius but also for the vitality that modern-day witchcraft enjoys. So, too, did J. Gordon Melton, a Methodist minister and founder of the Institute for the Study of American Religion. In a recent interview, he remarked that the whole neopagan movement owes its inception as well as its momentum to Gerald Gardner. "What today we call the modern witchcraft movement," declared Melton, "can all be dated to Gardner."

Doubts and debates about his sources notwithstanding, Gerald Gardner's influence on the course of the Wiccan revival is indisputable, as is his role as the spiritual father of the particular witchcraft "tradition" that today bears his name. While Gardner's methods showed more than a hint of the con artist, and his motives perhaps were mixed, his message was right for the times and found an enthusiastic audience on both sides of the Atlantic. Whether or not he rediscovered and revived an ancient path to wisdom, his followers were apparently able to see in his work a source of satisfying spiritual practice.

Moreover, as high priest of his own coven, Gerald Gardner was personally responsible for the initiation of dozens of new witches and for the creation of many new covens. These covens, in turn, bred other covens in a process that became known as hiving off and, in effect, created a kind of apostolic succession that could be traced back to Gardner's original coven. Other Gardnerian covens stemmed from self-starting witches who formed their own groups after they had read Gardner's books and had adopted his philosophy.

Not all witches pledge allegiance to Gardnerianism, however. Many of them profess a heritage that predates Gardner and model their rituals on various Celtic, Scandinavian, and

A Witch's Dictionary

Balefire: a ritual bonfire.

Book of Shadows: a witch's personal notebook of spells, rituals, and magical lore; also called a *grimoire.*

Charge: to transmit personal power into an object.

Charm: a charged object; an amulet is a charm said to ward off specific energies, and a talisman a charm to attract them.

Coven: a group of initiated Wiccans.

Craft, the: witchcraft; the Old Religion; see Wicca.

Deasil: clockwise, or sunwise; in ritual, the path of positive energies.

Divination: the art of discerning the unknown through tarot cards, crystal gazing, or the like.

Divine power: spiritual energy, the power of the Wiccan goddess and god.

Earth power: the energy in natural things; divine power made visible.

Elements: the Wiccan building blocks of the universe—earth, air, fire, and water; some traditions add a fifth element, spirit.

Esbat: Wiccan celebration of the full moon, occurring twelve or thirteen times a year.

Familiar: an animal with which a witch feels kinship, often in a magical partner relationship.

Invocation: a prayer at a coven gathering asking higher powers to make themselves known.

Magic: the art of changing consciousness or reality by nonphysical means, using either earth power or personal power.

Magic circle: the boundary of a sphere of personal power, within which Wiccans do rituals *(page 128).*

Neopagan: a practitioner of a contemporary nature religion, such as Wicca.

Old Ones, the: aspects of the deities that are invoked as guardians during Wiccan rituals; also called the Mighty Ones.

Pagan: from the Latin for *country dweller,* a member of a pre-Christian, magical, polytheistic religion.

Personal power: the power within each person, derived from the same source as divine power.

Sabbat: one of eight seasonal festivals *(page 123).*

Spell: a ritual invoking magic for helpful change.

Tradition, Wiccan: a denomination, or path, of Wiccan religious practice.

Wicca: a neopagan nature religion.

Widdershins: counterclockwise; many shun this direction as negative, but others use it to disperse negative energies or to undo a magic circle after a ritual.

Witch's tools: Wiccan ritual articles *(pages 120-121).*

Germanic traditions. Moreover, some of these so-called traditionals claim to be hereditary witches, born into the craft and fated to bequeath its secrets to their own offspring. Among them is a widely known feminist witch who calls herself Zsuzsanna, or Z, Budapest, and who is high priestess of the Susan B. Anthony Coven Number One, a group named after America's renowned women's-rights advocate. Z Budapest claims that her craft lineage can be traced back to her native Hungary and the year 1270. But she says that she herself was raised with an understanding of the craft only as craft, not as religion, and that she learned its basics from her mother, an artist who divined fortunes and allegedly used her magic powers to still the wind. It was not until years later, after Z had immigrated to the United States and discovered the works of writers such as Robert Graves and Esther Harding, that she initially recognized herself for the Wiccan she was.

Other self-described hereditary witches claim experiences similar to that of Z Budapest. They say the craft was for them a family affair until a chance encounter with Wiccan literature—often the books of Gerald Gardner or Margaret Murray, or those of such contemporary Wiccan authors as Starhawk, Janet and Stewart Farrar, or Margot Adler—led to the realization that they were a part of the wider world of Wicca. Lady Cybele, for example, a Wisconsin witch, says she grew up thinking that the craft was limited to a circle of family members. "It wasn't until college that I found out there were other people in the Craft," she confided to Margot Adler, "and I didn't know there were many of us until 1964 when my husband came running home from the library where he worked, bubbling with excitement, saying, 'There are more of us in the world.' " It turned out that Lady Cybele's husband had stumbled upon *Witchcraft Today,* and as they read the book together, she said, they were thrilled by their sense of familiarity with the ideas and practices described by Gerald Gardner.

Even if all such accounts were true, the accident of birth into a family of witches would be no guarantee that a particular child would eventually become privy to the secrets of the craft. In some instances the art skips a generation, usually because a witch determines that none of her own children have the right nature to adopt the craft. As a result, Wicca is rife with so-called grandmother stories, in which, as J. Gordon Melton puts it, "somebody pops up and says I was initiated by my grandmother who was a witch whose lineage goes way back." Few, if any, of these stories stand up to scrutiny, however, and many of them invite ridicule. Even Wiccans themselves are somewhat embarrassed about the glut of grandmother stories. "After a while," shrugged one Wiccan priest, "you realize that if you've heard one story about an old grandmother, you've heard six or seven just like it. You realize that the hereafter must be overpopulated with grandmothers."

Among the most notable of the grandmother stories is that told by the self-styled King of the Witches, Alexander Sanders, who claimed to have been initiated into the craft by his grandmother back in 1933, when he was just seven years old. But skeptics are quick to point out that Sanders's brand of witchcraft, known as the Alexandrian tradition, bears a strong resemblance to Gardner's. Indeed, many of Sanders's rituals are virtually indistinguishable from those of the Gardnerians, and this has prompted some observers to dismiss the Alexandrian tradition as merely a spin-off and not the legacy of some mysterious and conveniently deceased grandmother.

Many of those same skeptics took an equally dim view of the story of the celebrated English witch, Sybil Leek, who likewise claimed to have learned the craft at her grandmother's knee. In Melton's opinion, Leek, like Sanders, simply stretched the truth about her background. Attacks by doubters, however, did little to stem the tide of her popularity, and at the time of her death in 1983, Sybil Leek was one of the best-known witches on either side of the Atlantic Ocean. Leek was a prolific author, and during her lifetime she cranked out more than sixty books that spread the gospel of the Wiccan faith—and, not unintentionally, her own fame—around the world.

But more than all of Leek's books, what brought Wicca from England to the United States was the Gardnerian tradition itself, which crossed the Atlantic in 1964 as part of the spiritual baggage of two British expatriates. Raymond and Rosemary Buckland had already been settled for two years in New York's Long Island when, fired by their interest in the occult, they decided to write to Gardner at his home on the Isle of Man. That correspondence eventually led to a face-to-face meeting and a three-week crash course in witchcraft at Gardner's home. In that short time, the Bucklands, husband and wife, were transformed into Gardnerians, priest and priestess. They were among the last witches to be personally trained and anointed by Gardner before his death.

Returning to their adopted New York home, the Bucklands quickly got down to practicing what they had learned. Soon they established the first Gardnerian coven in the United States, and it, in time, hived off a number of other covens. These groups carried the Gardnerian gospel from coast to coast and into Canada. For a time, Rosemary Buckland, or Lady Rowen, as she was known to her fellow Wiccans, was crowned a witch queen by the covens she had set in motion. In the meantime, Ray Buckland, or Robat, as he had by then rechristened himself, took his cue from his mentor, Gerald Gardner, and published the first of several books he would write on the subject of witchcraft. These works helped make the craft accessible to many more prospective initiates, especially in its new home, where interest

Gerald Gardner (right) was already a famous Wiccan author when he used his magic wand to bless the marriage of two British witches in 1960. Gardner had retired to the Isle of Man, where he owned a witchcraft museum near the scene of two medieval witch burnings.

in Wicca boomed in the tolerant atmosphere of the late 1960s and 1970s.

Indeed, it was during the same years in which Ray and Rosemary Buckland set about bringing the Wiccan revival to North America that the occult began to take on what social anthropologist Tanya M. Luhrmann described as "countercultural chic." Writing in her 1989 book entitled *Persuasions of the Witch's Craft,* Luhrmann theorized that "the countercultural 1960s turned to occultism—to astrology, tarot and alternative healing and eating—because they were alternatives to the established culture: many people discovered tarot cards at about the same time they discovered beansprouts."

Ray Buckland remembers this period as an exciting time, during which more and more covens, and many different expressions of Wiccan belief, came into the open. Witches with highly personalized styles of practice were emboldened by the permissiveness of the period, and they finally felt free to stand up and be counted. At the same time, the transplanted Gardnerian tradition was thriving, and it strewed the seeds of new covens and splinter groups in every possible direction.

Modern witches visit the gloomy ruins of a twelfth-century chapel located on the Isle of Man. Home to Gerald Gardner in his last years, the island has a suitably mysterious history; its first ruler was said to have been a giant who could magically control the sea as well as the weather.

Zsuzsanna Budapest, founder of a feminist Dianic coven, holds aloft her ritual myrtle-tree broom. Regarding goddess worship as a means to empower women, Z—as Wiccans call her—has created rituals to stop sexual harassment and to aid in the pursuit of health and love.

church by federal, state, and local governments, seeks to provide common ground for these many paths. Circle Sanctuary calls itself an international exchange and contact service for Wiccans of all stripes. Many feminists, meanwhile, have found homes in one of the numerous Dianic covens that have sprung up since the 1970s. These groups take their name from Margaret Murray's notion of witchcraft as a Dianic cult, and they stress the worship of the goddess in their practices. There is even a correspondence course for would-be Wiccans that has attracted approximately 40,000 students.

Some of these groups, such as the Alexandrian tradition and a more recent hybrid that is called the Algard tradition, were chips off the old block, and they resembled the parent Gardnerian group in all but name. Others were more distant cousins, based on the teachings of Gerald Gardner, but with their own ideas thrown into the mix. Among these are Nova Wicca in Illinois, the California-based Georgian Wicca, and Maidenhill Wicca, which is headquartered in Philadelphia. Still others, including the Church of Y Tylwyth Teg, Pecti-Wita, and the Northern Way, looked back to the twilit and magic-bedecked past of Celtic, Scottish, and Norse legends for their inspiration.

The varieties of Wicca hardly end there, however; instead, they show a diversity that reflects the individualistic nature of witchcraft. Wicca is as open minded as it is eclectic. "We all connect to the Divine in different ways," says Selena Fox, herself the founder of a distinct Wiccan tradition. "There are many paths to the truth." In fact, Fox's own group, Circle Sanctuary, which is recognized as a Wiccan

But the rise of such "do-it-yourself" witches alarmed some of Wicca's earlier advocates, including Ray Buckland, who once lamented the advent of "homemade" religion. Yet, in 1973, prompted by what he saw as corruption of the craft, Buckland severed his own tie with Gardnerianism and devised a new set of practices, which he dubbed the tradition of Seax-Wica, or Saxon Wicca. In doing so, he also reversed his stand on self-taught witchcraft, and in *The Tree,* his Seax-Wica primer, included detailed instructions that allowed any reader "to initiate yourself as a Witch, and to start your own Coven."

With the seemingly contradictory announcement of a "new tradition" heard on every hand, Wicca entered a phase of divisive squabbling over seniority. In making his split from the Gardnerian tradition, Ray Buckland sought to distance himself from the fray. "While others fight over which is the oldest tradition," he announced with tongue-in-cheek pride, "I claim mine as the youngest!"

That was in 1973. Since then there has been such a profusion of Wiccan paths and covens that the honor of being the new kid on the block has at times been a momentary distinction. Likewise, with such a plethora of rites and denominations, Wicca itself has become a slippery faith to define. Efforts to formulate a creed acceptable to all who call themselves Wiccans have so far proved futile, despite a strongly felt need to publicly proclaim a set of beliefs to officially dissociate the craft from Satanism. The Council of American Witches, a group of representatives from many Wiccan sects, in 1974 stitched together a document bravely entitled "Principles of Wiccan Belief." No sooner was it ratified, however, than the consensus it represented came apart at the seams and dissension set in among the council's members. The following year a new consortium that today embraces some seventy Wiccan groups ratified the Covenant of the Goddess, a more durable charter that was intentionally patterned after that of the Congregational church. Although the covenant included a code of ethics and guaranteed the autonomy of its signatory covens, it stopped short of defining Wicca. "We could not define what a Witch is in words," the covenant concedes, "because there are too many differences."

Many witches contend that those very differences are part of Wicca's appeal. Indeed, even within a particular tradition, different covens may hold contrasting beliefs and practice dissimilar rituals. This state of affairs is satisfactory to most witches, who see no reason why Wiccans should be any less diverse in their beliefs than the many denominations of Christians.

Even in the absence of an official creed, however, a large number of witches do subscribe to the so-called Wiccan rede, or law: "An ye harm none, do what ye will." The source of this permissive adaptation of the Christian golden rule is not precisely known, but it has been in existence at least since the time of Gerald Gardner. In the words of the United States Army's own *Handbook for Chaplains*, the Wiccan rede is "generally interpreted as meaning that a practitioner can do whatever he or she wishes with the psychic abilities developed through the practice of the Craft, as long as he or she does not harm anyone with these powers." As an additional safeguard against the misuse of witchy powers, many covens also endorse something called the threefold law, which is another time-honored maxim. This adage wags a gnarled finger at witches and warns them that "what good you do returns to you threefold; what harm you do also returns to you threefold."

Given the difficulty of pigeonholing witchcraft or of pinning down a concise list of beliefs common to all Wiccans, a description of the characteristics that make a modern witch a witch is necessarily an approximation. It can safely be said, however, that the vast majority of witches believe in reincarnation, revere nature, worship a multifarious and all-pervasive deity, and incorporate ritual magic into that worship.

In addition, there are few witches who would dispute the encapsulation of basic beliefs that author Margot Adler offered in *Drawing Down the Moon*. "The world is holy," she wrote. "Nature is holy. The body is holy. Sexuality is holy. The mind is holy. The imagination is holy. You are holy. A spiritual path that is not stagnant ultimately leads one to the understanding of one's own divine nature. Thou art Goddess. Thou art God. Divinity is . . . as much within you as without."

Underlying such beliefs are three philosophical assumptions, which more than any other characteristics, link modern witchcraft and neopaganism to corresponding practices in the ancient world. The first assumption is animism, or the idea that such supposedly inanimate objects as rocks and trees are imbued with spirits all their own. A second common thread is pantheism, which holds that divinity is part and parcel of nature. And the third characteristic is polytheism, or the conviction that divinity is both multiple and diverse.

Taken together, these beliefs comprised a general outlook toward the divine that animated the pre-Christian world. In the words of historian Arnold Toynbee, "divinity was inherent in all natural phenomena, including those that man had tamed and domesticated. Divinity was present in springs and rivers and the sea; in trees, both the wild oak and the cultivated olive-tree; in corn and vines; in mountains; in earthquakes and lightning and thunder." God, or divinity, was felt to be everywhere, in everything; "plural, not singular; a pantheon, not a unique almighty superhuman person."

Writer and witch Starhawk echoes much the same theme when she observes that witchcraft "is not based on dogma or a set of beliefs, nor on scriptures, or a sacred book revealed by a great man. Witchcraft takes its teachings from nature and reads inspiration in the movements of the sun, moon and stars, in the flight of birds, in the slow growth of trees and in the cycles of the seasons."

But Starhawk also acknowledges that it is the polytheistic aspect of Wicca—the worship of "the Triple Goddess of birth, love and death and of her Consort, the Hunter, who is Lord of the Dance of Life"—that most sets modern witchcraft apart from the mainstream of Western religion. Even so, many Wiccans disagree on whether their god and goddess are mere symbols, actual entities, or powerful primal images—what psychologist Carl Jung called archetypes—

deeply rooted in the human subconscious. Witches are also equally divided on what appellations to give their deities. As expressed in the incantation of high priestess Morgan McFarland at the Arlington Street Church, names for the god and goddess abound. They range from Cernunnos, Pan, and Herne for the male side of the godhead, to Cerridwen, Arianrhod, and Diana for the female side. In fact, there are so many different names, drawn from so many cultures and traditions, that McFarland was not far off the mark when she told her audience that the goddess "shall be called a million names."

By whatever appellation, it is the goddess who in the majority of Wiccan sects takes precedence over the god. Her exalted status is reflected in such titles as the Great Goddess and the Great Mother. Indeed, to Starhawk and many other witches, the worship of a supreme female deity is the very essence of witchcraft and a force that "underlies the beginnings of all civilizations."

Starhawk recalls that "Mother Goddess was carved on the walls of paleolithic caves and sculpted in stone as early as 25,000 B.C." and contends that women were often the leaders in goddess-centered cultures thousands of years ago. "For the Mother," she writes, "great stone circles, the henges of the British Isles, were raised. For Her the great passage graves of Ireland were dug. In Her honor sacred dancers leaped the bulls in Crete. Grandmother Earth sustained the soil of the North American prairies, and Great Mother Ocean washed the coasts of Africa."

In Starhawk's view, the goddess is no distant and domineering God the Father, prime mover of the earth below and remote ruler of a heaven beyond. Instead, she is a wise and valued friend who is in and of this world. Starhawk likes to think of the goddess as the breath of the universe and yet utterly real. "People often ask me whether I believe in the Goddess," writes Starhawk. "I reply, 'Do you believe in rocks?' "

Certainly strength and permanence are the obvious

Famed British witch Sybil Leek was said to be casting a spell when this 1966 photograph was taken; she had been robbed while visiting St. Louis and was conjuring a harsh fate for the culprit. In a more benign mood (right), Leek blesses the countryside in the New Forest region of southern England, reputedly the home of the revival of witchcraft in the twentieth century.

implications in the image of the goddess as rock. However, it is the goddess in her guise as a many-faceted and ever-changing divinity, as a mystery woman who reveals herself by degrees and sometimes not at all, that seems to appeal most to witches. For that reason, the female deity is often symbolized by the inconstant moon, with a different phase—whether waxing crescent, full moon, or waning crescent—corresponding to the three aspects of the Triple Goddess: Maiden, Mother, and Crone.

The ceremony known as Drawing Down the Moon *(page 131)* builds on this symbolism and represents one of the most mystical of Wiccan rituals. In this ceremony, the high priestess of a coven invokes the power of the Great Mother and then takes on the role of the goddess herself. As part of the celebration, the high priestess recites the invocation that is called the Charge of the Goddess, in which she summons each one of her witches to her side. "I who am the beauty of the green earth, and the white Moon among the stars, and the mystery of the waters, and the desire of the heart of man, call unto thy soul," she beckons. "Arise and come unto me."

Among those answering the call of the goddess today are an increasing number of feminists. Many of them joined one or another of the hundreds of Dianic covens that had formed by the 1980s, making feminist witchcraft the fastest growing segment of the craft. Most of these covens exclude men, and Z Budapest, a leader in the feminist witch movement, goes so far as to call witchcraft the Wimmin's Reli-

gion. She sees it as a faith in which men should play no part. Some other feminist Wiccans agree and even take the idea one step further by asserting that all women are witches solely by virtue of their gender.

The attraction of witchcraft to feminists is understandable, since they believe, as Margot Adler contends, that a witch is "an extraordinary symbol—independent, anti-establishment, strong and proud. She is political, yet spiritual and magical." At the same time, modern witchcraft has developed as a singularly female expression of spirituality—with faith vested in a passionate and nurturing goddess and rituals that acknowledge and even embrace the cyclic nature of a woman's life. As such, the Wiccan religion is devoid of the patriarchy and hierarchy that have come to characterize Christianity. "It is a women's religion," one writer declared, "a religion of the earth, vilified by patriarchal Christianity and now, finally, reclaimed."

Moreover, in reclaiming the goddess, many of today's feminist witches are also staking claim to what they see as their rightful heritage. They are reaching back across the dim centuries to a time when a woman was not just the tender of the family hearth but also the guardian of ritual and the custodian of tribal memory. Writer Monique Wittig captured the spirit when she reminded her female readers: "There was a time when you were not a slave, remember that. You walked alone, full of laughter, you bathed barebellied. You know how to avoid meeting a bear on the

track. You know the winter fear when you hear the wolves gathering. But you can remain seated for hours in the tree-tops to await morning. You say there are no words to describe this time, you say it does not exist. But remember. Make an effort to remember. Or, failing that, invent.''

Thus some feminists view witchcraft as an attempt to remedy the historical and cultural amnesia they say has been imposed on women throughout centuries of male domination. For others, especially those who, in the purest sense of the word *witch,* are bending Wiccan reality to create their own woman-centered traditions, witchcraft is closer to invention. ''What the feminist Witches hold is a new, yet ancient, essence of pure worship,'' two witches once wrote in a Wiccan journal. ''They hold the future. And they come, as the North Wind: with the chill of change, and the freshness of rebirth.''

Modern-day feminism only partly accounts for the expansion of Wicca in the 1970s and 1980s. The craft is populated with thousands of witches who are neither feminist nor even female, and these followers offer a multitude of per-

sonal reasons for responding to the call of the goddess. In fact, with the number of Americans practicing some form of neopaganism today, there would seem to be room enough in the Wiccan faith to accommodate witches of every background and persuasion.

Some of them, no doubt, are escapists who have opted out of society, spiritual dilettantes bored enough to seek their excitement in the offbeat and privileged enough to have the opportunities to find it. Yet most witches, in writer Susan Roberts's estimation, are not the idle rich but ''middle-class Americans who, on the surface, live quietly and unobtrusively in the mainstream of American life.'' Roberts further observes that while witches generally defy categorization, they do tend to be nonconformists and tend to have retained ''that simple faith most of us believe to be the special province of children.''

Other observers have reported similar findings. British anthropologist Tanya Luhrmann, for one, notes that a large number of the witches she questioned regarding the allure of witchcraft cited such motivating forces as a ''need to be childlike, to marvel at nature and to re-experience an imag-

Illuminated by an artist friend of the owner, this Wiccan Book of Shadows, or grimoire, flouts the old rule that a magic journal must contain only the witch's own handwriting. In these safer days, many Wiccans photocopy others' grimoires or type their own onto computer disks.

The Wheel of the Wiccan Year

Wiccans speak of the year as a wheel; their calendar is a circle, signifying that the cycle of seasons turns endlessly. Almost evenly spaced around the Wiccan Wheel of the Year are the eight Wiccan feast days, or sabbats. These are distinct from esbats, the twelve or thirteen occasions during a year when covens gather to celebrate the full moon. The four minor sabbats, in fact, are solar holidays, milestones in the sun's yearly journey around the skies. The four major sabbats celebrate the earth's agricultural cycle of seedtime, growth, harvest, and rest.

The sabbat cycle is a retelling and celebration of the age-old story of the Great Goddess and her son and consort, the Horned God. Wiccan sects cherish a host of variations on this myth; one traditional version follows, embodying many Wiccan beliefs about death, rebirth, and the faithful return of cycles.

Yule, a minor sabbat, is the feast of the winter solstice (about December 22), marking not only the longest night of the year but the start of the sun's return. At this time, the story goes, the goddess gives birth to the god, represented by the sun; she then rests through the cold months, which belong to the infant god. At Yule, Wiccans light fires or candles to welcome the sun, and they decorate with holly and mistletoe—red for the sun, green for eternal life, white for purity.

Imbolc (February 1), a major sabbat also called the Feast of Candles, cele-

brates the first stirrings of spring, the sprouting of seeds unseen under the ground. Longer days show the power of the boy god. Wiccans end winter's confinement with purification rites and light all manner of fires, from white candles to great bonfires.

At the minor sabbat of the spring equinox (about March 21), the exuberant goddess is awake and strewing the earth with fertility. Wiccans color eggs, plant seeds, and plan new enterprises.

At Beltane, or May Day (May 1), another major sabbat, the god attains manhood as the goddess's power to bring forth fruit peaks. Stirred by nature's energies, they mate and she conceives. Wiccans enjoy a flower festival, often including a dance around a maypole, a fertility symbol.

Midsummer (about June 21) is the longest day and calls for bonfires hon-

oring the goddess and the god. It is also an occasion for handfastings, Wiccan weddings, at which the newlyweds jump over a broom. The season's major sabbat is Lugnasadh (pronounced "loon-sar"), on August 1, which marks the first harvest and the promise of ripening fruits and grains. Early grain is baked into sun-shaped loaves. As the days shorten, the god weakens, even as the goddess feels their child in her womb. At the autumn equinox (about September 22), the god prepares to die and the goddess is at her most bountiful. Wiccans give thanks for the harvest, symbolized by the cornucopia.

Just opposite the riotous flowering of Beltane on the Wheel of the Year stands the major sabbat of Samhain (pronounced "soe-en"), October 31, when all that flowered is dying or dormant. The sun grows fainter, and the god is dying. Aptly, this is the Wiccan New Year, embodying the faith that every death brings rebirth through the goddess. In fact the next feast, Yule, celebrates anew the birth of the god.

The coincidence of these festivals to Christian holidays, and the similarities between Wiccan and Christian symbols, say many anthropologists, are not accidental, but prove the preexistence of the pagan beliefs. For Christian authorities contending with older religions during Europe's Dark Ages, converting established holidays by giving them new Christian meanings eased the acceptance of the new faith.

prenticeship, lend credence to Luhrmann's suggestion that embracing Wicca is more a process of self-persuasion than conversion. "Becoming involved with magic," she writes, "is like entering a world of 'let's pretend.' " The novice encounters a great many new and exotic ideas, and he or she must gradually arrive at decisions about whether or not they have value. The craft does not demand immediate commitment and there exists no prepackaged set of beliefs for the novice to put into practice. Instead, the new student is simply allowed to experiment and play, testing the waters as it were.

In this manner, the practice of witchcraft precedes belief, during what often becomes a protracted period of soul-searching. Particularly because the Wiccan creed flies in the face of convention, many newcomers need to take time for a gradual growth of belief. Throughout this exploratory phase, the novice discovers new ways of viewing the world. Luhrmann suggests that this slow and often idiosyncratic evolution of personal philosophy may explain, at least to some extent, why witches find it so difficult to agree on a common creed.

For those who wind up embracing Wicca, the ritual comes to seem less theatrical and more meaningful. Eventually, Luhrmann observes, "magic seems practical, reasonable, commonsensical, and the experience of engaging in magic an enjoyable part of their life."

For many Wiccans, an important milestone along this path of growing belief is initiation as a witch. Some new practitioners perform a solitary ceremony of self-initiation, an affirmation of beliefs and of dedication to the goddess and god. Other Wiccans are inducted into the religion and into a coven at the same time, joining a group that may range in size from three to thirty members. Whether simple or elaborate, the attendant ritual *(see page 128)* is an outward signal of the novice's transition from explorer to devotee. Initiation often includes a blessing of the new witch's tools *(pages 120-121),* and when the ritual is completed, a solemn oath of secrecy seals the ceremony—and the lips of its participants.

In Salem, Massachusetts, once the scene of witch trials and executions, modern witches gather together for a sabbat with Laurie Cabot (center), who in 1975 was named the official witch of Salem. The eerie blue lightning-like streak that appears at the bottom of this photograph was attributed by Eastman Kodak to static electricity on the film, but Cabot disagreed. The energy was present in the room, she insisted, and it formed "the perimeter of our magic circle."

counselor for the Salvation Army in Pascagoula, Mississippi, until her firing in August 1987. Dodge, who acknowledged being a witch, was dismissed from her job after she was caught using the photocopying machine at her office to duplicate pages of Wiccan rituals. She sued her former employer on grounds of religious discrimination, and the Salvation Army countered in court that the reason for the firing was that she had violated organizational policy against personal use of photocopies. Dodge's attorney tried to the matter in perspective way: "If she was a Christian and would have been using this copy machine, wh would have cared? would have bee machine from a Betty Crocker cookbook, would have minded." The case went to tri 88, and a federal judge ruled that Dodge was indeed a violation of her to worship as she pleased. The $1.25 suit was later settled out of court for an undisclosed but substantial sum.

Secrecy is, in fact, a source of comfort to witches, for even today many of them still live in fear. Misconceptions about witchcraft and misinterpretation of its beliefs make the followers of Wicca targets of vandalism, discrimination, and job dismissals.

One of the more celebrated recent trials involving witchcraft was a lawsuit filed by Jamie Kellam Dodge, a

Secular hassles are harsh reality for many modern-day Wiccans. Selena Fox and the members of her Circle Sanctuary, for example, live in a farming community near Madison, Wisconsin, and at one point, they had to wage a two-year legal battle to win recognition as a church from their town and county governments—this in spite of the fact that the state of Wisconsin and the Internal Revenue Service had

long since granted them church status. The dispute started as a routine zoning hearing, but it became so entwined in the age-old bugaboos about witchcraft as a form of Satanism that the local press began referring to the matter as the "witch hunt." Speaking about Fox and requesting anonymity, one member of a neighboring church told a reporter, "She scares me. What they do is not normal." And a county official described Circle Sanctuary as an "anti-church."

The response of Fox's coven was to hold an open house, after which at least some visitors to Circle Sanctuary's 200-acre retreat conceded that the group's activities, which include Wiccan weddings and planetary healing ceremonies, were anything but evil. "I've gone to her rituals to see what's going on," admitted a local probation officer, who served on a Wisconsin state committee on cults and gangs. "They are a very open, almost childlike group. The problem is, people see witchcraft, Satanism and the occult as all the same thing."

Confusion of witchcraft with Satanism has at times extended to the highest levels of government. In 1985, citing widespread concern about "the growth of cults, Satanism, witchcraft, sorcery and the like," Senator Jesse Helms attached to an otherwise routine appropriations bill an amendment that would have denied tax-exempt status to Wiccan groups. The bill in fact was ratified by the Senate but was later killed by a joint House-Senate conference committee after neopagan groups mounted a massive letter-writing campaign.

In the face of such opposition and in an effort to place Wicca on the same legal footing as other religions, some witches and neopagans have sought strength in numbers, forming networks to provide mutual support. Among the new umbrella organizations are Circle Sanctuary, the Covenant of the Goddess, and the Witches Anti-Defamation League. In joining forces in this manner, some witches have had to throw back the accustomed security blanket of secrecy under which the majority of their colleagues take shelter. A few of them welcome the change, feeling that the usual reticence of witches has in the past often led to apa-

thy. "A lot of Christians only go to church on Christmas and Easter," observes Selena Fox, "and a lot of pagans only come out on Halloween."

Fox herself is among the most prominent and active Wiccan leaders. As part of what she calls her ministry, she has made frequent appearances on television talk shows and given numerous lectures at colleges and elsewhere. Closer to home, she once worked side by side with other area churchwomen as a volunteer for the Red Cross after a tornado devastated the nearby town of Barneveld in June 1984. Her efforts to give Wicca a respected public face finally paid off in 1988 when she was invited to speak at a conference of the World Council of Churches. Fox remembers the event, which took place in Toronto, as one of the high points of her ministry.

But the struggle to win legitimacy for the craft may have a price. The institutionalization of witchcraft raises in the minds of some practitioners the specter of a breakdown in craft values. Particularly troubling is the growing clamor for a paid clergy, which has risen in some factions of Wicca. Traditionalists feel that such a change would transgress the craft's own dictates against spreading the word for money. "One thing I don't want to see," says Gerald Gardner's original high priestess, Doreen Valiente, "is Witchcraft becoming too much of an organized religion."

That prospect seems remote, however, despite the remarkable growth that the craft has enjoyed in recent decades. For one thing, the proliferation of varied "traditions" makes centralization unlikely. Nevertheless, many experts do forecast continued expansion for Wicca, and J. Gordon Melton, among others, has detected the emergence of a "mature, sophisticated leadership" that may ensure the craft's future.

As for the problems inherent in that growth, it is likely that a religion whose central invocation, the Charge of the Goddess, calls for "mirth and reverence" will be able to take in stride many real-world concerns. "Being alive is really rather funny," one priestess told anthropologist Tanya Luhrmann. "Wicca is the only religion that captures this."

Drawing Down the Moon

Wiccans identify the ever-changing moon—waxing, full, and waning—with their Great Goddess in her varied aspects as Maiden, Mother, and Crone. Thus it is that a ceremony intended to bring the moon's magical power to earth, called Drawing Down the Moon, is the essence of goddess worship and a key rite in the Wiccan liturgy.

When meeting for one of the year's twelve or thirteen esbats, or full-moon celebrations, members of the Athanor Fellowship gather around the magic circle to direct their psychic energies through their high priest, seen here kneeling in the center, to their high priestess, who stands with arms upraised toward the night sky. The concentration of their energy will help the priestess, so they believe, to "draw the moon into herself" and become an embodiment of the goddess.

"The time of the full moon is a time of very intense psychic tension in general," explains High Priest Arthen. Drawing Down the Moon is aimed at harnessing the tension. The ritual, says Arthen, "helps the priestess to go into a very deep trance, in which she can experience visions, or speak words that often are of relevance to people in the coven."

The cups in the priestess's hands hold water, the element that symbolizes and is ruled by the moon. The coven members say that this water becomes "psychically charged" with the power coursing through her. Each witch will drink some of it at the end of the ritual, in what High Priest Arthen terms a sacrament.

Many groups draw down the moon in its other phases as well as when it is full. They try to tap the power of the waxing moon to promote growth and beginnings, and that of the waning or dark moon to seal the endings of things that ought to end. And while most groups consider the ceremony a way to honor the Great Goddess, many forgo stylized ritual, simply taking a moment when the moon is full to meditate on that Wiccan deity.

Raising the Cone of Power

"Magic," says High Priest Arthen, "is working with psychic forces to make changes." Part of a witch's training, he points out, is to learn to use psychic energy, and one primary technique, a ritual performed at almost every coven meeting, is Raising the Cone of Power. Like most other witch activities, it takes place within a magic circle. For this ritual especially, says Arthen, the magic circle is visualized as not just a circle but "a dome, or bubble, of psychic energy—a way to hold the power in before we do something with it."

In their efforts to generate energy for a cone of power, witches use many means, including dancing, meditating, and chanting. To "mold" the power they claim to produce, they gather around the magic circle, stretch their arms toward the earth, and gradually raise them, as seen here, toward a focal point above the circle's center. When the coven's leader feels that the group's energy is at a peak, she or he commands the members, "Send it now!" Then the witches all visualize the energy rising, as a cone, out of the circle and traveling onward to its previously determined destination.

The cone's target may be someone who is ill or in need or perhaps coven members who want assistance in their magical work. But the destination can also be less specific. In keeping with the craft's grounding in nature, the cone of power may be sent, says Arthen, "to help redress the environmental crises we find ourselves in."

Feasting through the Wiccan Year

Wiccan rituals are not all somberness and solemnity. "We mix mirth and reverence," says Arthen. The eight sabbats that highlight the witches' year *(page 123)*—honoring th   ey and the earth's rhyth   re occasions for most festive of salute to spring that first of May. For Beltane the p EarthSpirit gather to enjoy a traditiona, maypole frolic, as seen here.

The maypole dance, an old fertility rite, begins as a ritualized game involving the kind of strong sexual symbolism that characterizes many witchcraft ceremonies. The women of the coven dig a hole in which the obviously phallic maypole is to be planted. But when the men approach, carrying the pole, they are confronted by a ring of women surrounding the hole as if defending it. In a symbolic courtship, the women teasingly open and close the circle at different places as the males run around the outside with the pole, seeking a way in.

"Eventually," says High Priest Arthen, "the men are allowed to bring the pole in and plant it in the hole, and then both men and women cement it in place with earth." Finally, the witches perform their interweaving dance around the maypole, crossing and recrossing one another's paths so that the bright ribbons they hold are plaited around the pole. "The ritual binds female and male energy together," Arthen explains, "so that fertility will abound."

Believing that each sabbat brings the peak of its own kind of psychic and earthly energies, witches perform sabbat rituals even if they must do so alone. In recent years, however, Wiccans have gathered in ever-larger numbers for sabbat celebrations; attendance at EarthSpirit's festivals has grown sevenfold in about a decade.

Like other religious groups, Wiccan communities celebrate significant steps in individual and family life, including birth, death, marriage, which they call handfasting, and the naming of children. Earth-Spirit is recognized as a church by the Commonwealth of Massachusetts, Arthen says, and therefore its handfasting rite can confer legal marriage. Often, however, handfasting is used to create not a legal marriage but a bond recognized only by Wiccans. If a couple thus joined decide to separate, their bond can be undone by another Wiccan ceremony, known as handparting.

Central to handfasting are the blessing of the couple's union *(right)* and the ritual binding of their clasped hands *(left)*—the step that gives the rite its name and long ago yielded the familiar phrase for marriage, "tying the knot." The colorful band that fastens the pair together is one they have created from three strands of fiber or leather, representing the bride, the groom, and their relationship. For weeks or months before this day, the couple have regularly taken time—at each new moon, perhaps—to sit together, braid part of the cord, and talk over the interweaving of their two lives, in love, work, friendship, sex, and children.

Children born to witches are presented to the coven in a naming ritual called a child blessing, or—in old Scots—saining. Many sainings include the planting of a tree, which may be fertilized by the child's placenta or umbilical cord. By a similar ceremony known as a magical saining, which usually comes before initiation *(page 128)*, apprentice witches declare the names by which they choose to be known within the craft.

ACKNOWLEDGMENTS

The editors would like to thank the following individuals and institutions for their assistance in the preparation of this volume.

Andras Corban Arthen, the Athanor Fellowship, and the EarthSpirit Community, Medford, Massachusetts; François Avril, Curator, Bibliothèque Nationale, Paris; Professor Hans Bender, Director, Institut für Grenzgebiete der Psychologie und Psychohygiene, Freiburg, West Germany; Lucy B. Burgess, Department of Rare Books, Cornell University, Ithaca, New York; Charles Butler, ECUMENECON, Silver Spring, Maryland; Pinuccia Di Gesaro, Bolzano, Italy; Dr. James Duke, Fulton, Maryland; Gertrude Foster, Falls Village, Connecticut; Luisa Francia, Munich, West Germany; Ursula Hagen-Jahnke, Deutsche Bundesbank, Frankfurt, West Germany; Robert Held, Certaldo, Italy; Christoph Hinkeldey, Mittelalterliches Kriminalmuseum, Rothenburg, West Germany; M. A. Howard, Cardigan, Wales; Aidan Kelly, Santa Barbara Centre for Humanistic Studies, Santa Barbara, California; Pat Kenney, Silver Spring, Maryland; Heidi Klein, Bildarchiv Preussischer Kulturbesitz, West Berlin; Gabrielle Kohler, Archiv für Kunst und Geschichte, West Berlin; Kevin McCurley, Washington, D.C.; Dr. Franz Machilek, Chief of Staatsarchiv, Bamberg, West Germany; Dr. J. Gordon Melton, Santa Barbara, California; Dr. Manfred van Rey, Stadtarchiv, Bonn, West Germany; Helen Ann Mins Robbins, Saugerties, New York; Dr. Rossell Hope Robbins, Saugerties, New York; Dr. Bernhard Schemmel, Staatsbibliothek, Bamberg, West Germany; Professor Wolfgang Schild, University Bielefeld, Bielefeld, West Germany; Holly H. Shimizu, Washington, D.C.; Heidi Staschen, Hamburg, West Germany; Dr. Rolf Streichardt, Institut für Grenzgebiete der Psychologie und Psychohygiene, Freiburg, West Germany; Robert Tine, Rome; Jim Tyler, Department of Rare Books, Cornell University, Ithaca, New York; Doreen Valiente, Brighton, England; Dr. Rüdiger Vossen, Museum für Völkerkunde, Hamburg, West Germany; Marion Weinstein, Earth Magic Productions, New York; Dr. Robert Zink, Chief of Stadtarchiv, Bamberg, West Germany.

BIBLIOGRAPHY

Adler, Margot, *Drawing Down the Moon*. Boston: Beacon Press, 1986.

Barthell, Edward E., Jr., *Gods and Goddesses of Ancient Greece*. Coral Gabels, Fla.: University of Miami Press, 1971.

Baskin, Wade, *The Sorcerer's Handbook*. New York: Philosophical Library, 1974.

Bremness, Lesley, *The Complete Book of Herbs*. New York: Viking Penguin, 1988.

Buckland, Raymond, *Buckland's Complete Book of Witchcraft*. St. Paul: Llewellyn Publications, 1986.

Budge, E. A. Wallis, *Amulets and Superstitions*. New York: Dover Publications, 1978 (reprint of 1930 edition).

Bulfinch, Thomas, *Bulfinch's Mythology*. Comp. by Bryan Holme. New York: Viking, 1979.

Campbell, Joseph:
The Hero with a Thousand Faces. Princeton, N.J.: Princeton University Press, 1949.
The Masks of God: Occidental Mythology. New York: Penguin Books, 1964.
The Masks of God: Primitive Mythology. New York: Penguin Books, 1969.

Campbell, Joseph, with Bill Moyers, *The Power of Myth*. Ed. by Betty Sue Flowers. New York: Doubleday, 1988.

Caro Baroja, Julio, *The World of the Witches*. Transl. by O. N. V. Glendinning. Chicago: University of Chicago Press, 1964.

Carroll, David, *The Magic Makers: Magic and Sorcery through the Ages*. New York: Arbor House, 1974.

Cavendish, Richard, ed., *Man, Myth & Magic: The Illustrated Encyclopedia of Mythology, Religion and the Unknown*. New York: Marshall Cavendish, 1985.

Clebsch, William A., *Christianity in European History*. New York: Oxford University Press, 1979.

Clifton, Chas S., "A Goddess Arrives." *Gnosis*, fall 1988.

Cohn, Norman, *Europe's Inner Demons: An Enquiry Inspired by the Great Witch-Hunt*. New York: New American Library, 1975.

Cunningham, Scott:
Cunningham's Encyclopedia of Magical Herbs. St. Paul: Llewellyn Publications, 1988.
The Truth about Witchcraft Today. St. Paul: Llewellyn Publications, 1988.
Wicca: A Guide for the Solitary Practitioner. St. Paul: Llewellyn Publications, 1989.

Daraul, Arkon, *Witches and Sorcerers*. London: Frederick Muller, 1962.

Davidson, H. R. Ellis, *Gods and Myths of Northern Europe*. Baltimore: Penguin Books, 1964.

Davidson, James West, and Mark Hamilton Lytle, *After the Fact: The Art of Historical Detection*. New York: Alfred A. Knopf, 1982.

Di Gesaro, Pinuccia, *Streghe*. Bolzano, Italy: Praxis 3, 1988.

Eisler, Riane, *The Chalice and the Blade*. San Francisco: Harper & Row, 1988.

Encyclopedia of Witchcraft & Demonology. London: Octopus Books, 1974.

Farrar, Janet, and Stewart Farrar, *The Life & Times of a Modern Witch*. London: Judy Piatkus, 1987.

Fitter, Richard, and Alastair Fitter, *The Wild Flowers of Britain and Northern Europe*. London: Collins, 1974.

Fletcher, Robert, M.D., *The Witches' Pharmacopoeia*. Baltimore: Friedenwald, 1896.

Fosberry, John, transl., *Criminal Justice through the Ages*. Rothenburg ob der Tauber, West Germany: Mediaeval Crime Museum, 1981.

Fraser, Antonia, *The Weaker Vessel*. New York: Alfred A. Knopf, 1984.

Friedell, Egon, *A Cultural History of the Modern Age*. Transl. by Charles Francis Atkinson. Vol. 1. New York: Alfred A. Knopf, 1964 (reprint of 1930 edition).

Gardner, Gerald B., *Witchcraft Today*. London: Jarrolds, 1968.

Gassier, Pierre, *Goya*. Transl. by James Emmons. Cleveland: World Publishing, 1955.

Graves, Robert:
Greek Myths. New York: Doubleday, 1981.
The White Goddess. New York: Creative Age Press, 1948.

Grimal, Pierre, ed., *Larousse World Mythology*. New York: G. P. Putman's Sons, 1968.

Hamilton, Edith, *Mythology*. Boston: Little, Brown, 1942.

Hansen, Harold A., *The Witch's Garden*. Transl. by Muriel Crofts. York Beach, Maine: Samuel Weiser, 1983.

Harrison, Michael, *The Roots of Witchcraft*. Secaucus, N.J.: Citadel Press, 1973.

Hart, George, *A Dictionary of Egyptian Gods and Goddesses*. London: Routledge & Kegan Paul, 1986.

Hauschild, Thomas, Heidi Staschen, and Regina Troschke, *Hexen*. Hamburg, West Germany: Hochschule für bildende Künste, 1979.

Held, Robert, *Inquisition* (exhibition catalog). Florence, Italy: Qua D'Arno, 1985.

"Helms Seeks Restrictions on Tax Exemptions for Witchcraft and Satanism Groups." Amendment No. 705. *Congressional Record*, September 26, 1985.

Howey, M. Oldfield, *The Cat in the Mysteries of Religion and Magic*. Rutland, Vt.: Charles E. Tuttle, 1981.

Hoyt, Charles Alva, *Witchcraft*. Carbondale, Ill.: Southern Illinois University Press, 1981.

"In Search of Meaningful Ritual." *Utne Reader*, November-December 1987.

Jacob, Dorothy, *A Witch's Guide to Gardening*. New York: Taplinger, 1964.

Jong, Erica, *Witches*. New York: Harry N. Abrams, 1981.

Judge, Joseph, "Minoans and Mycenaeans." *National Geographic*, February 1978.

Kelly, Aidan, *Inventing Witchcraft*. Santa Barbara, Calif.: Santa Barbara Centre for Humanistic Studies, 1989.

King, Francis X., *Witchcraft and Demonology*. New York: Exeter Books, 1987.

Kohn, Bernice, *Out of the Cauldron: A Short History of Witchcraft*. New York: Holt, Rinehart and Winston, 1972.

Kors, Alan C., and Edward Peters, eds., *Witchcraft in Europe 1100-1700: A Documentary History*. Philadelphia: University of Pennsylvania Press, 1972.

Larner, Christina, *Witchcraft and Religion: The Politics of Popular Belief*. Ed. by Alan Macfarlane. Oxford, England: Basil Blackwell, 1984.

Larousse Encyclopedia of Mythology. New York: Putnam, 1968.

Leach, Maria, ed., *Funk & Wagnalls Standard Dictionary of Folklore, Mythology and Legend*. San Francisco: Harper & Row, 1984.

Lehane, Brendan, and the Editors of Time-Life Books, *Wizards and Witches* (The Enchanted World series). Alexandria, Va.: Time-Life Books, 1984.

Lewis, Arthur H., *Hex*. New York: Pocket Books, 1970.

Luhrmann, T. M., *Persuasions of the Witch's Craft: Ritual Magic in Contemporary England*. Cambridge, Mass.: Harvard University Press, 1989.

MacCulloch, John Arnott, *The Mythology of All Races*. Vol. 2. New York: Cooper Square, 1964.

Mackay, Charles, *Extraordinary Popular Delusions and the Madness of Crowds*. Vol. 1. New York: Crown, 1980 (reprint of 1841 edition).

McMurray, Scott, "Real Witches Today Don't Stew Newts, at Least Not in Wisconsin." *The Wall Street Journal*, October 31, 1988.

McNeill, William H., *A World History*. New York: Oxford University Press, 1979.

Melton, J. Gordon, interview with Greg Maniatis (researcher), Time-Life Books, Alexandria, Va., July 5, 1989.

Mercatante, Anthony S., *The Magic Garden: The Myth and Folklore of Flowers, Plants, Trees, and Herbs*. New York: Harper & Row, 1976.

Midelfort, H. C. Erik, *Witch Hunting in Southwestern Germany 1562-1684*. Stanford, Calif.: Stanford University Press, 1972.

Murray, Margaret Alice, *The Witch-Cult in Western Europe*. London: Oxford University Press, 1962 (reprint of 1921 edition).

Newall, Venetia, *The Encyclopedia of Witchcraft & Magic*. New York: Dial Press, 1974.

O'Connell, Margaret F., *The Magic Cauldron: Witchcraft for Good and Evil*. New York: S. G. Phillips, 1975.

Peffer, Randall S., "Massachusetts' North Shore Harboring Old Ways." *National Geographic*, April 1979.

Peters, Edward, *The Magician, the Witch and the Law*. Philadelphia: University of Pennsylvania Press, 1978.

Ravensdale, Tom, and James Morgan, *The Psychology of Witchcraft*. New York: Arco, 1974.

Richardson, Katherine W., *The Salem Witchcraft Trials*. Salem, Mass.: Essex Institute, 1983.

Robbins, Rossell Hope, *The Encyclopedia of Witchcraft and Demonology*. New York: Bonanza Books, 1981.

Roberts, Susan, *Witches U.S.A.* New York: Dell, 1971.

Rosen, Barbara, *Witchcraft*. London: Edward Arnold, 1969.

Ross, Anne:
Pagan Celtic Britain: Studies in Iconography and Tradition. London: Routledge and Kegan Paul, 1967.
The Pagan Celts. London: B. T. Batsford, 1986.

Russell, Jeffrey Burton:
A History of Witchcraft, Sorcerers, Heretics and Pagans. London: Thames and Hudson, 1980.
Witchcraft in the Middle Ages. Secaucus, N.J.: Citadel Press, 1972.

Ryan, Mary P., *Womanhood in America: From Colonial Times to the Present*. New York: New Viewpoints, 1979.

Sallmann, Jean-Michel, *Les Sorcières Fiancées de Satan*. Paris, France: Gallimard, 1989.

Schickel, Richard, and the Editors of Time-Life Books, *The World of Goya 1746-1828* (Time-Life Library of Art series). Alexandria, Va.: Time-Life Books, 1968.

Scott, A. F., *Witch, Spirit, Devil*. London: White Lion, no date.

Sharkey, John, *Celtic Mysteries: The Ancient Religion*. London: Thames and Hudson, 1975.

Shepard, Leslie, ed., *Encyclopedia of Occultism & Parapsychology*. 3 vols. Detroit: Gale Research, 1984.

Sjöö, Monica, and Barbara Mor, *The Great Cosmic Mother*. San Francisco: Harper & Row, 1987.

Stuart, Malcolm, ed., *The Encyclopedia of Herbs and Herbalism*. New York: Crescent Books, 1979.

Summers, Montague:
The History of Witchcraft and Demonology. London: Routledge and Kegan Paul, 1973 (reprint of 1926 edition).
The Werewolf. Secaucus, N.J.: Citadel Press, 1966.

Summers, Montague, transl., *The Malleus Maleficarum of Heinrich Kramer and James Sprenger*. New York: Dover, 1941.

Thomas, Keith, *Religion and the Decline of Magic*. New York: Charles Scribner's Sons, 1971.

Walker, Barbara G.:
The Woman's Dictionary of Symbols and Sacred Objects. San Francisco: Harper & Row, 1988.
The Woman's Encyclopedia of Myths and Secrets. San Francisco: Harper & Row, 1983.

Warner, Rose, "Circle Sanctuary Sect Commutes with Divine through Nature." *The Dodgeville Chronicle*, January 14, 1988.

Wedeck, H. E., and Wade Baskin, *Dictionary of Pagan Religions*. New York: Philosophical Library, 1971.

Weinstein, Marion, *Positive Magic: Occult Self-Help*. Custer, Wash.: Phoenix Publishing, 1981.

PICTURE CREDITS

The sources for the pictures are given below. Credits from left to right are set off by semicolons, from top to bottom by dashes.

Cover: Artwork by Bryan Leister 7: Roger Ressmeyer/ Starlight. 8: The National Maritime Museum, London. 9: The Hulton-Deutsch Collection, London. 12: Michael Holford, Loughton, courtesy the British Museum, London. 14: The Mary Evans Picture Library, London. 15: Archivio Fotografico die Musei Capitolini, Rome. 16: Erich Lessing, Culture and Fine Arts Archives, Vienna—Barry Iverson, courtesy Egyptian Museum, Cairo. 17: Ekdotiki Athenon, Athens. 18: From *A History of Witchcraft: Sorcerers, Heretics, and Pagans*, by Jeffrey B. Russell, Thames and Hudson, London, 1980, courtesy Sotheby's. 19: Bibliothèque Nationale, Paris. 21: Scala/Art Resource, New York. 22: Dosso Dossi, *Circe and Her Lovers in a Landscape*, National Gallery of Art, Washington, D.C., Samuel H. Kress Collection. 23: Courtesy the Trustees of the British Museum, London. 24: Scala, Florence/Art Resource, New York, courtesy Museo Archeologico, Ferrara, Italy. 26, 27: O. Vaering, Oslo. 28, 29: Lennart Larsen, Danish National Museum, Copenhagen. 31: Pamela Harper. 32, 33: Pamela Harper, except upper right Allen Paterson, Royal Botanical Gardens, Ontario. 34: Pamela Harper, except upper left Harry Smith, Chelmsford, Essex. 35: Allen Paterson, Royal Botanical Gardens, Ontario; Pamela Harper—Pamela Harper; Jack Potter. 36: Pamela Harper, except lower right Smith/ Polunin Collection, Chelmsford, Essex. 37: Pat Brindely, Cheltenham, Gloucester; Allen Paterson, Royal Botanical Gardens, Ontario—Pamela Harper. 38: Pamela Harper, except lower right Harry Smith, Chelmsford, Essex. 39: Pamela Harper (2)—Allen Paterson, Royal Botanical Gardens, Ontario; Holly H. Shimizu, United States Botanic Gardens.

41: Roger Ressmeyer/Starlight. 42, 43: Claus Hansmann, Munich. 44-46: Courtesy Cornell University Library. 47: Giraudon, Paris. 48: General Research Division, New York Public Library, Astor, Lenox and Tilden Foundation, courtesy Cornell University Library—from *Picture Book of Devils, Demons and Witchcraft*, by Ernst and Johanna Lehner, Dover Publications, New York, 1971. 52-54: Archiv für Kunst und Geschichte, West Berlin. 55: Claus Hansmann, Munich. 56, 57: Bildarchiv Preussischer Kulturbesitz, West Berlin, courtesy Prado, Madrid. 58: The Lambeth Palace Library, London. 59: Jean-Loup Charmet, Paris. 60: From *The Encyclopedia of Witchcraft and Demonology*, by Rossell Hope Robbins, Bonanza Books, New York, 1981; courtesy Cornell University Library. 61: The Hulton-Deutsch Collection, London—from *The Stratford-upon-the-Avon Library 6: Witchcraft*, edited by Barbara Rosen, Edward Arnold Publishers, London, 1969; the Bettmann Archive. 62: Giancarlo Costa, Milan. 63: Bildarchiv Preussischer Kulturbesitz, West Berlin; from *The Stratford-upon-the-Avon Library 6: Witchcraft*, edited by Barbara Rosen, Edward Arnold Publishers, London, 1969. 64: Courtesy Cornell University Library. 65: From *Inquisition, a Catalogue of the Exhibition of Torture Instruments Shown in Various European Cities*, © 1983 by Robert Held, Certaldo (FI), Italy, except lower left Bildarchiv Preussischer Kulturbesitz, West Berlin. 67: Bibliothèque Nationale, Paris. 68: From *Le Musée des supplices*, by Roland Villeneuve, Éditions du Manoir, Paris, 1971. 70: Archiv für Kunst und Geschichte, West Berlin. 71: Paul Dijkstra, courtesy the Museum de Heksenwaag, Oudewater, the Netherlands; Foundation Witch Weighhouse Oudewater, the Netherlands. 73-75: Courtesy the Essex Institute, Salem, Massachusetts. 76, 77: Courtesy the Essex Institute, Salem, Massachusetts, except title page, Rare Books and

Manuscripts Division, the New York Public Library, Astor, Lenox and Tilden Foundation. 78: Courtesy Cornell University Library. 79: Courtesy the British Library, London. 80: Danvers, Massachusetts Archival Center—the Mansell Collection, London. 81: Bibliothèque Nationale, Paris. 82, 83: Ingeborg Limmer, courtesy Staatsbibliothek, Bamberg; Archiv für Kunst und Geschichte, West Berlin—from *Inquisition: A Catalogue of the Exhibition of Torture Instruments Shown in Various European Cities*, © 1983 by Robert Held, Certaldo (FI), Italy (2). 84, 85: From *Inquisition: A Catalogue of the Exhibition of Torture Instruments Shown in Various European Cities*, © 1983 by Robert Held, Certaldo (FI), Italy, except top right Rare Books and Manuscript Division, New York Public Library, Astor, Lenox and Tilden Foundation, courtesy Cornell University Library. 86, 87: From *Inquisition: A Catalogue of the Exhibition of Torture Instruments Shown in Various European Cities* © 1983 by Robert Held, Certaldo (FI), Italy (3); Archiv für Kunst und Geschichte, West Berlin. 88: Staatsbibliothek, Bamberg. 89-95: Artwork by Barry Moser. 97: Roger Ressmeyer/Starlight. 98: Courtesy Martin Memorial Library, York, Pennsylvania. 99: Henry Groskinsky. 100, 101: Patricia A. Paterno. 103: Associated Press, London. 105: UPI/Bettman Newsphotos. 106: Ruth Bayer, London. 109: Popperfoto, London. 110, 111: Camera Press, London. 112: Los Angeles Times Photo. 113: Jack and Betty Cheetham/Magnum. 114: The Bettmann Archive. 116, 117: AP/Wide World Photos; Associated Press, London. 118: Patricia A. Paterno. 119: From *Wicca: A Guide for the Solitary Practitioner*, by Scott Cunningham, Llewellyn Publications, St. Paul, 1989. 120, 121: Henry Groskinsky. 123: Artwork by Kim Barnes of Stansbury, Ronsaville and Wood, Inc. 124, 125: Nathan Benn © 1979 National Geographic Society. 127-137: Henry Groskinsky.

INDEX

Time-Life Books is a division of Time Life Inc.,
a wholly owned subsidiary of
THE TIME INC. BOOK COMPANY

TIME-LIFE BOOKS

Managing Editor: Thomas H. Flaherty
Director of Editorial Resources: Elise D. Ritter-Clough
Director of Photography and Research: John Conrad Weiser
Editorial Board: Dale M. Brown, Roberta Conlan, Laura
Foreman, Lee Hassig, Jim Hicks, Blaine Marshall, Rita
Thievon Mullin, Henry Woodhead

PUBLISHER: Joseph J. Ward

Associate Publisher: Ann M. Mirabito
Editorial Director: Russell B. Adams, Jr.
Marketing Director: Anne C. Everhart
Director of Design: Louis Klein
Production Manager: Prudence G. Harris
Supervisor of Quality Control: James King

Editorial Operations
Production: Celia Beattie
Library: Louise D. Forstall
Computer Composition: Deborah G. Tait (Manager),
Monika D. Thayer, Janet Barnes Syring, Lillian Daniels

Library of Congress Cataloging in Publication Data
Witches and Witchcraft / by the editors of Time-Life
Books.
  p. cm.—(Mysteries of the unknown)
  Includes bibliographical references.
  ISBN 0-8094-6392-X   ISBN 0-8094-6393-8 (lib. bdg.)
  1. Witchcraft—History. 2. Witchcraft.
  I. Time-Life Books.   II. Series.
  BF1566.W75 1990   89-28091
  133.4'3—dc20   CIP

MYSTERIES OF THE UNKNOWN

SERIES EDITOR: Jim Hicks
Series Administrator: Myrna Traylor-Herndon
Designer: Herbert H. Quarmby

Editorial Staff for *Witches and Witchcraft*
Associate Editors: Susan V. Kelly (pictures);
Robert A. Doyle (text)
Text Editors: Janet Cave, Margery A. duMond
Researchers: Constance Contreras, Sarah D. Ince,
Elizabeth Ward
Staff Writer: Marfé Ferguson Delano
Assistant Designer: Susan M. Gibas
Copy Coordinators: Mary Beth Oelkers-Keegan, Colette
Stockum
Picture Coordinator: Katherine Griffin
Editorial Assistant: Donna Fountain

Special Contributors: Lesley Coleman (London, picture re-
search); Cheryl Binkley, Patti H. Cass, Sheila M. Green,
Gregory A. Maniatis, Patricia A. Paterno (research);
George Daniels, Norman Draper, Dónal Kevin Gordon, Pe-
ter W. Pocock, Daniel Stashower, Bryce Walker (text);
John Drummond (design); Hazel Blumberg-McKee (index).

Correspondents: Elisabeth Kraemer-Singh (Bonn), Christina
Lieberman (New York), Maria Vincenza Aloisi (Paris), Ann
Natanson (Rome).
Valuable assistance was also provided by Mirka Gondicas
(Athens); Angelika Lemmer, Wanda Menke-Glückert
(Bonn); Robert Kroon (Geneva); Judy Aspinall, Christine
Hinze (London); Simmi Dhanda, Deepak Puri (New Delhi);
Elizabeth Brown (New York); Ann Wise (Rome).

Consultants:
Marcello Truzzi, general consultant for the series, is a
professor of sociology at Eastern Michigan University. He
is also director of the Center for Scientific Anomalies Research (CSAR) and editor of its journal, the *Zetetic Scholar*.
Dr. Truzzi, who considers himself a "constructive skeptic"
with regard to claims of the paranormal, works through
the CSAR to produce dialogues between critics and propo-
nents of unusual scientific claims.

Margot Adler is the author of *Drawing Down the Moon:
Witches, Druids, Goddess-Worshippers, and Other Pagans in
America Today*. She is a reporter for National Public Radio
and also lectures widely on witchcraft, paganism, and
women's spirituality.

Selena Fox is the founder and high priestess of Circle
Sanctuary, an international Wiccan church headquartered
in Wisconsin. A leading Wiccan religious-freedom activist,
she conducts workshops and seminars on the Wiccan religion and mysticism and has written on the subjects for
several periodicals and books.

Other Publications:

THE NEW FACE OF WAR
HOW THINGS WORK
WINGS OF WAR
CREATIVE EVERYDAY COOKING
COLLECTOR'S LIBRARY OF THE UNKNOWN
CLASSICS OF WORLD WAR II
TIME-LIFE LIBRARY OF CURIOUS AND UNUSUAL FACTS
AMERICAN COUNTRY
VOYAGE THROUGH THE UNIVERSE
THE THIRD REICH
THE TIME-LIFE GARDENER'S GUIDE
TIME FRAME
FIX IT YOURSELF
FITNESS, HEALTH & NUTRITION
SUCCESSFUL PARENTING
HEALTHY HOME COOKING
UNDERSTANDING COMPUTERS
LIBRARY OF NATIONS
THE ENCHANTED WORLD
THE KODAK LIBRARY OF CREATIVE PHOTOGRAPHY
GREAT MEALS IN MINUTES
THE CIVIL WAR
PLANET EARTH
COLLECTOR'S LIBRARY OF THE CIVIL WAR
THE EPIC OF FLIGHT
THE GOOD COOK
WORLD WAR II
HOME REPAIR AND IMPROVEMENT
THE OLD WEST

*For information on and a full description of any of the Time-
Life Books series listed above, please call 1-800-621-7026 or
write:*
Reader Information
Time-Life Customer Service
P.O. Box C-32068
Richmond, Virginia 23261-2068

This volume is one of a series that examines the history
and nature of seemingly paranormal phenomena. Other
books in the series include:

TIME
LIFE ®